Aberfeldy's Railway

C J Stewart

The Birks of Aberfeldy

The Braes ascend like lofty wa's,
The foaming stream, deep roaring fa's,
O'erhung wi' fragrant spreading shaws,
  The Birks of Aberfeldy

The hoary cliffs are crowned wi' flowers,
While o'er the Linn the burnie pours,
And rising, weets, wi' misty showers,
  The Birks of Aberfeldy

Robert Burns 1759-1796

Aberfeldy was a typical branch line terminus. Most of the time nothing happened. Occasionally someone would arrive to collect or deliver a parcel or to enquire about train times. There was a bit more activity around the newsagent stand. But when a train was due, a small group would assemble ready to welcome returning loved ones or greet visitors. There would be hustle and bustle for a few minutes as people went on their way. The locomotive would uncouple and retreat to the shed in the distance, as it has done here, to take on water or possibly coal. Perhaps it would shunt a few wagons into the sidings on the left. Then as the time for the next departure drew near, the reverse would happen until the train left and all was quiet again. This scene dates from the 1950s but shows what had happened since the line opened in 1865 and would continue into the 1960s.

© C J Stewart 2012
ISBN: 978 0 95454856 8

All rights reserved. No part of this publication may be reproduced, stored in a retrieval system or transmitted, in any form or by any means, electronic, mechanical, photocopying, recording or otherwise, without the prior written permission of the publisher.

Published by the Highland Railway Society : www.hrsoc.org.uk.

Printed by Information Press, Eynsham, Oxfordshire, OX29 4JB

Front cover : the Aberfeldy branch as many will recall it from the 1950s. Ex-Caledonian 0-4-4 tank no.55217 arrives with a mixed train on 1st September 1961. The single passenger coach sufficed but there is a good load of wagons, including several with coal for the local fireplaces.   (Colour-Rail.com)

Rear cover upper : Watercolour of Logierait Bridge by Sir Anthony Wheeler OBE PPRSA which was painted to help with fund raising for the restoration of the bridge.   (Logierait Bridge Co.)

Rear cover lower : The branch train waits at Ballinluig for passengers from the connecting main line. The locomotive is a Type 2 of what was later known as Class 26.   (Colour-Rail.com)

Contents

Introduction 5

False Hopes 7

Real Beginnings 11

The Penultimate Hurdle 15

Constructing the Line 21

Initial Impact 29

Changes and Benefits 33

Operating the Line 37

Fatalities, Fires, Flood and Findings 45

End of the Line 49

Memories of the Final Decade 55

Lasting Reminders 59

Bibliography 63

Aberfeldy in 1912, with a train waiting to leave for Ballinluig. The locomotive is an 0-6-4 tank designed for banking trains up the climb to Druimuachdar and the coaches are typical hand-me-downs from main line use.

The other end of the branch was Ballinluig, on the main line from Perth to Inverness, seen in April 1965. Here trains for Aberfeldy used the platform on the left, which had its own loop on the far left so that branch engines could run round their trains without interfering with traffic on the main line. A local train from Blair Atholl can be seen arriving at the up platform on the right. These main line platforms were very long and extended beyond a level crossing on the other side of the footbridge. With few houses nearby, nearly all passengers just spent a few minutes here so the wooden buildings were quite basic. The Highland Railway did not see fit to replace them with the substantial stone structures to be found at larger places such as Pitlochry.

(Graham Maxtone collection)

Introduction

The *Perthshire Advertiser* of 6th July, 1865 contained a feature describing the opening of the Aberfeldy Branch Line of railway, a section of which is as follows:-

In this age of wonders, the impossibilities of one year become the realities of the next. Schemes that exist only in the brain of some so-called moonstruck individuals, are, a year or two after their accomplishment, looked upon with as little unconcern as an old "Defiance" mail coach. Through similar phases the Inverness and Perth Junction railway has passed. When the undertaking was proposed a few years ago, many, not unwise in their generation shook their heads, and explained satisfactorily to themselves how the projected line was a hairbrained affair from beginning to end. Like certain men who went to spy an enemy's country, they saw Anak-like giants of difficulties, which human effort could never overcome. The many mighty bens, beetling rocks, deep passes and ravines, together with the desolate, barren wilds through which the line was to run, all these were thought to be insuperable obstacles. Yet, notwithstanding these difficulties, the Inverness and Perth line was constructed, was opened, and has prospered beyond the expectations of even the schemers themselves. To such an extent has the line prospered that the directors already see to stand still will be greatly to their loss, and so they intend to push as many branch lines as possible throughout these "desolate" highland parts. The success of the main line has proved that this will be to the interest of shareholders. Accordingly on the 16th January 1864 the first sod was cut of a branch line to Aberfeldy; and on Saturday last, the government inspector (Captain Rich RE) tested the line, and pronounced it safe for public traffic. On Monday the line was opened for passenger and goods, and now there is communication daily by rail between Aberfeldy and all parts of Scotland and England.

To attempt a description of the country through which the line passes would be, in the present case, futile. To our reader in the highland district the attempt would be like taking coal to a miner, or knives to a cutler. To all others who have not seen the district we say, take a trip to Aberfeldy; for the beauties of Strathtay, like many other beauties in this world of ours must be seen to be fully appreciated.

The so-called impossibilities, difficulties and obstacles regarded as insuperable and beyond human effort were overcome and the Aberfeldy branch did open for traffic on 3rd July, 1865. This book is intended, hopefully, to illustrate how this was achieved, show who were involved in promoting the venture, detail the construction and other difficulties met, indicate who and how people were affected and describe the effect on the communities in Strathtay during its existence.

My thanks go to many people who have helped with the preparation of this book, including Messrs Allen Gordon & Co., Mrs J Adamson, Mrs L Fischbacher, Mrs S Menzies, Mrs M Murdoch, Mr N McCandlish, Mr G Gregory and Mr M J Dorward. My son has used his computer skills to redraw original plans and my daughter typed the manuscript; the staff of the National Archives of Scotland, the National Library of Scotland, the Blair Castle Archivist and the staff of the A K Bell Library, Perth, have been very helpful. Finally thanks to the Highland Railway Society for publishing the book and to Keith Fenwick for preparing it for publication.

The road bridge at the west end of Grandtully station gave a good view of the station. This photograph from before 1914 shows the staff lined up with handcarts waiting for a train. In the distance, coal is being unloaded into a horse-drawn cart. The signal box in the far distance controlled access to the sidings. (HRS collection)

The other intermediate stopping place was Balnaguard, a simple halt opened by the LMS on 2nd December 1935 to serve the adjacent hamlet. It must have been popular as some trains in the 1950s stopped here but missed out Grandtully. (Keith Fenwick)

False Hopes

The early Victorian years witnessed significant transformation and transition. With the Napoleonic wars almost a generation past, a new era of peace and prosperity dawned, bringing among other things mobility, huge social change and the expansion of industry. All this was coupled with and mainly due to the growth of the railways. At this time and in common with most parts of Highland Scotland the Strathtay area was, however, predominantly a land based economy. Travel for individuals would either be by foot or on horse, transport for groups by carriage or coach and conveyance of goods by cart; additionally the lack of bridges meant river crossings were chiefly by ferry. Communication, therefore, was slow, poor and unreliable, greatly hindering any prospect of economic and social development in the area. It is not surprising that local opinion was so galvanised in their desire to be connected to the new and proposed railway network from Perth to Inverness that the following petition was delivered to the Marquess of Breadalbane, the principal landowner of the area.

To the most noble the Marquess of Breadalbane

The Petition of the Inhabitants of Aberfeldy

Humbly Sheweth

That your petitioners being all much interested in having the benefit of Railway Communications are glad to see that the landed proprietors, farmers and others in the district are taking steps with a view to having the branch line to Aberfeldy formed and opening simultaneously with the line to Pitlochry.

For this in the opinion of your petitioners is of the very greatest importance to Aberfeldy for if Pitlochry were to have the benefit of Railway Communications before Aberfeldy, not only would tourists be attracted to Pitlochry to the neglect of Aberfeldy, and the great loss and injury of lodging houses, and hotel keepers and posting establishments in the whole district, but the trade of Rannoch and Foss would all find its way to Pitlochry and be retained there – that the village would extend and soon afford such increased facilities for the wants of Trade of the District, as to make it a formidable rival to Aberfeldy and put a stop to the rapidly rising importance of the District's latter place and prevent it becoming, as it otherwise would, a country town capable of supplying the wants of the wide district around it – thus injuring Aberfeldy and at the same time depriving the district of the advantages which a thriving and larger town would afford.

That your petitioners believe that the tenantry and inhabitants of Aberfeldy are quite disposed to take shares to the extent of their ability.

That your petitioners therefore beg most respectfully to solicit that your lordship will be pleased to promote the undertaking by every means in your power.

And your petitioners will ever pray.

The above petition being signed by more than 160 Aberfeldy citizens ranging from J. McLaren, Minister; A. Carmichael, Union Bank of Scotland; John Robertson, Labourer and Alex Kettle, Carter.

The Marquess did, in response, become the leading proponent and principal shareholder of the proposed Strathtay & Breadalbane Railway Company, the said company to connect with the newly proposed Perth & Inverness railway at Ballinluig. Although a separate company, it was, nonetheless,

ACCOUNT OF OUTLAY BY ARCHIBALD REID, WRITER, PERTH ON BEHALF OF THE STRATHTAY AND BREADALBANE RAILWAY COMPANY

1845							
Nov	4	Paid for use of Room at George Hotel when allocating shares in proposed undertaking		£	"	5	"
	5	Paid drosky hire and expenses with Mr Tasker going over line with reference to certain difficulties about carrying the line past Grandtully		£	1	4	"
	10	Paid hires and travelling and incidental expenses posting parliamentary notices on the church doors of Dull, Weem, Little Dunkeld and Logierait – 3 days each time – 12 days in all		£	16	3	6
		Paid beadles fees		£	1	"	"
		Paid hires and personal expenses for Mr A Scott for six days while employed taking up the book of reference viz:-					
	17	Hire to Birnam	£ " 15 "				
		Tolls, driver and hostler	" 8 6				
		Hire to Aberfeldy	1 7 6				
		Tolls, driver and hostler	" 10 "				
	18	Gig hire from the line to Aberfeldy	" 5 "				
		Toll, hostler and postboy	" 5 6				
		Paid a guide and a person to carry plans books etc	" 6 "				
	19	Gig hire to and from line	" 5 "				
		Toll, hostler and postboy	" 5 6				
		Paid guide and person to carry plans	" 6 "				
	20	Gig hire all day	" 10 "				
		Horse keep at Sketewen	" 2 6				
		Postboy, tolls and hostler	" 5 6				
		Guide and man to carry plans	" 6 "				
	21	Gig all day	" 10 "				
		Keep of horse	" 2 6				
		Postboy, hostler and tolls	" 5 6				
		Paid guide	" 4 "				
	22	Gig hire to Logierait and back to Aberfeldy	" 10 "				
Tolls, ferry and postboy			" 5 6				
		Horse keep	" 2 6				
		Paid guide	" 4 "		8	2	"
		Mr Scott's personal expenses these six days			6	6	"
		My own expenses, hire, tolls, postboy etc going from Perth this day to meet Mr Scott and revise and adjust the whole reference			1	19	"
	25	Paid carriage of parcel to me in Edinburgh with M.S. book of reference			"	1	"
	29	Paid Sheriff Clerk fee on depositing parliamentary plans etc			1	1	"
Dec	19	Paid postage to Mr Bowie Campbell W.S. with notices to be sent to Lord Lauderdale and Lord John Hay			"	1	2
	21	Paid postage with notices to Grahame and Weem			"	1	2
		Paid postage to Mr Pagan, Cupar, Fife			"	"	10
		Paid postage to Mr Kerr, Dundee			"	"	6
		Paid do to Mr Steel, Glasgow			"	"	6
		Paid do to Revd Mr Kennedy			"	"	6
	26	Paid chaise hire to Birnam for self and assistant to serve notices on lessees and occupiers			1	2	6
		Carried forward		£	37	18	8

dependant on the other railway obtaining parliamentary consent and being built.

In order to obtain an Act specific and detailed protocols and procedures have to be followed; amongst those are the submission of plans to accord with prescribed requirements and the necessity for the publication of notices in various named locations.

Firstly, therefore, engineers were appointed, the line was surveyed and two plans Nos 1 and 2 of the Strath Tay & Breadalbane Railway in the county of Perth were produced. These were drawn to the prescribed scale of 4 inches to 1 mile and also indicated a limit of deviation of 110 yards (half a furlong) on both sides of the line. Shown too were the various numbered plots in their respective parishes of Logierait, Little Dunkeld, Dull and Weem to denote the affected owners who were listed in the Book of Reference which accompanied the submission to Parliament.

This proposed route was in fact broadly similar to that which was ultimately built with two significant differences; Aberfeldy station was intended to be located near the gasworks beside the junction of Chapel Street and Market Street and the proposed route in the Grandtully area was shown as passing through the Haugh of Grandtully to the north of the village, between what is now the A827 and the River Tay. Since some evidence exists to suggest that an extension to Kenmore was mooted, the intended station site would have facilitated that option; being situated at the low end of Aberfeldy it gave a more straightforward access to the carseland westwards to the Loch Tay area.

Secondly and perhaps of more interest was the work undertaken to ensure the publication, distribution and serving of the notices, required by parliamentary standing orders as a condition to the submission of a bill to Parliament. The extract opposite clearly illustrates what is involved in this process but more pertinently paints a picture not only of mid-nineteenth century life in the Strathtay area but the meticulous record and book keeping by the legal profession of that era.

A further four pages of detailed expenses followed on from the extract, some of a similar nature to that shown but also listing expenses incurred in trips to London to witness proceedings in the House of Lords, various printing and paper costs, the costs for newspaper advertising and finally a bill for interest to 20th July 1849 amounting to £65.7.8d. The final account of outlay totalled £514.19.4d.

The capital of the railway was £120,000, with powers to borrow one third of that, i.e. £40,000. Land had to be purchased within 3 years of the passing of the Act and construction completed within 7 years.

It is perhaps appropriate to comment on a few points; firstly the picture painted of 19th century travel, the whole undertaking being done on foot, gig or ferry and with the necessity for guides; secondly warning of the difficulties that would be encountered between Grandtully and Aberfeldy and lastly to emphasise that Mr Reid displayed the renowned characteristics of sagacity and canniness typical of a traditional Scottish lawyer by ensuring that the kirk beadles too received a fee!

Despite all this effort having been diligently and properly undertaken it was, sadly, to no avail as the *Perthshire Courier* of 21st May 1846 reported

> *Perth and Inverness Railway – The decision of the committee has rendered the proposed meeting of shareholders, under the sessional orders, unnecessary, the Bill having been thrown out. This resolution was to come to solely from the present state of experience, as to severe gradients of considerable length over great altitudes, and it is not to be taken as giving an opinion against the formation of the line, should the experience of the working of the railways now in progress of a similar character, support the principle on which the Perth and Inverness was proposed to be constructed.*

However, the Strathtay & Breadalbane Railway Bill was not opposed and, as there were so many railway bills to be considered that year, it was automatically enacted. The Company was set up but as there would be no connection at Ballinluig, it was of little purpose. The only solution was to carry on southwards as the succeeding article in the same newspaper goes on to explain:-

Strathtay and Breadalbane Railway – This railway, which proposed to unite Aberfeldy with the Perth and Inverness line at Ballinluig, on the east side of the Tay, about 5 miles above Dunkeld, is to go on notwithstanding the loss of the latter. There will only be that additional line of five miles to be formed to connect it with Midland junction at Dunkeld, and thereby secure a connection with Perth and Dundee; and as nearly the whole stock is in the hands of the Marquess of Breadalbane, with whom the line originated, there is no doubt of its going forward. It will be a great accommodation to the Perthshire highlands, the more so that the Perth and Crieff direct and the Perth and Inverness lines have been for the present stopped.

A Bill was duly submitted in late 1846 to extend the line down to Dunkeld, where it would meet a branch of the Scottish Midland Junction which had been authorised in 1845. Additional capital of £150,000 and borrowing powers of £50,000 were sought. However, the financial support for new railways had now evaporated and the Bill was withdrawn after the second reading in the House of Commons. This still left the Strathtay & Breadalbane Railway Company in existence and it applied for an extension of time for another two years when the original powers expired in 1849. Eventually the company was wound up.

The Scottish Midland Junction did not proceed with its Dunkeld branch due to the same financial pressures and to disputes with local landowners but retained the power to do so. Eventually, a separate company, the Perth & Dunkeld Railway, was authorised to build the branch and it opened in 1856.

Thus these initial dreams were not to be realised and another fifteen to twenty years elapsed before the hopes and aspirations of the Strathtay area could be brought to fruition.

An early view of Aberfeldy from the south with the railway station in its original condition in the foreground. If the Strathtay & Breadalbane as authorised in 1846 had been built, its terminus would have been on the other side of the houses in the right-hand half of the photograph. (HRS collection)

Real Beginnings

Those described as not unwise in their generation because they considered that severe gradients of considerable length over great altitudes were impossibilities that could not be overcome in time relented. No doubt the ability of civil engineers to design solutions that conquered Shap and Beattock and, equally, the capacity of their mechanical counterparts to build locomotives that too overcame such obstacles played a significant part in this regard. It must be said, in fairness, that this was a totally new technology, possessing no historical precedent, indeed initially perceived opinion not too far distant considered that travel in excess of fifteen miles per hour would result in death by asphyxiation. At last, however, movement took place and the first step of many took place with the issue of a parliamentary notice.

This notice dated 8th November 1860 was to advise Parliament of the intention to submit for consideration a Bill to incorporate a company which inter alia would make and maintain a railway from Forres junction to Birnam, near Dunkeld, with a branch to Aberfeldy. Much general and generic requirements relating to such an activity were listed therein and the penultimate paragraph states that all relevant plans, sections, books of reference and notices would be published or displayed in all the prescribed publications and locations. Finally the last paragraph stated the following:-

> *And notice is hereby also given, that on or before the 23rd day of December next, printed copies of the intended Bill will be deposited in the Private Bill office of the House of Commons.*

To construct a railway an Act of Parliament is necessary. It creates a statutory company to undertake the building of those lines specifically detailed in the submission; each unique Act also embraces and incorporates several enabling acts viz:- The Companies Clauses Consolidation (Scotland) Act, 1845; The Lands Clauses Consolidation (Scotland) Act, 1845; The Railways Clauses Consolidation (Scotland) Act, 1845 and The Lands Clauses Consolidation Acts Amendment Act 1860. The inclusion of these other Acts allows for new companies to compulsory acquire land and to extract tolls (fares).

The Inverness & Perth Junction Railway Act, 1861, was thus published on 22 July 1861; much of it is dry legal terminology but the following hopefully gives an explanation of the aims of the company and some of the rules under which it operated. Part of the preamble illustrates the objectives:-

> *Whereas the making of a railway from the town of Forres in the county of Elgin, and communications there with the Inverness and Aberdeen junction railway, to the village of Birnam near Dunkeld in the county of Perth, there to communicate with the Perth and Dunkeld railway with a branch diverging therefrom near the village of Ballinluig to Aberfeldy, will be of great local and public advantage: And whereas the estimated cost of constructing the said railway is Six hundred and fifty four thousand Pounds: And whereas the persons herein-after named, with others, are willing at their own expense to carry the said undertaking into execution.*

Section 26 listed the following as first directors:

> *His Grace the Duke of Athole, His Grace the Duke of Sutherland, The Most Noble the Marquis of Breadalbane, The Right Honourable the Earl of Seafield, The Honourable Thomas Charles Bruce, Sir Alexander Penrose Gordon Cumming Baronet, Sir Robert Menzies Baronet, Alexander McIntosh*

of McIntosh, Alexander Mathieson, Eneas William Mackintosh, Evan Baillie, William Fraser Tyler, George Loch, Colonel Hugh Inglis, and Alexander Inglis Robertson shall be the first directors of the company.

The quorum of a meeting of directors was to be five. The powers for the compulsory purchase of land lasted four years and the railway had to be completed within six years from the passing of the Act, at which time the powers granted to the company for executing the railway would cease except for the railway as then completed.

The rates for tolls (fares and charges) for the conveyance of goods and passengers were also decreed by legislation and the Act contains many sections relating to the subject; section 42 gives the details:-

It shall be lawful for the company to demand any tolls for the use of the railway not exceeding the following; (that is to say)

First, in respect of the tonnage of all articles conveyed upon the railway, or any part thereof, as follows:-

For all dung, compost, and all sorts of manure, lime and limestone, and all undressed materials for the repair of the public roads or highways, per ton per mile not exceeding one penny halfpenny; and if conveyed in carriages belonging to the company, an additional sum per ton per mile not exceeding one penny:

For all coal, coke, culm, charcoal and cinders, all stones for building, pitching, and paving, all bricks, tiles, slate, clay, sand, ironstone, and iron ore, pig iron, bar iron, rod iron, hoop iron, and all other similar descriptions of wrought iron and iron castings not manufactured into utensils or other articles of merchandise, per ton per mile not exceeding two pence; and if conveyed in carriages belonging to the company, an additional sum per ton per mile not exceeding one penny:

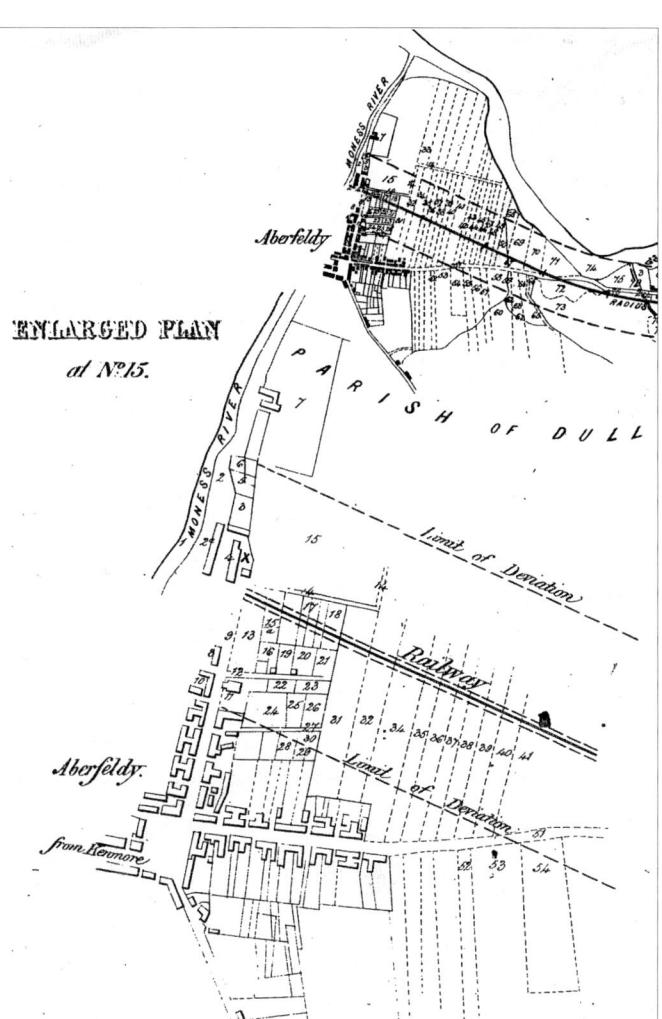

Details of Aberfeldy from the plans which were deposited with the I&PJ Bill. This shows where it was originally intended to locate the terminus.

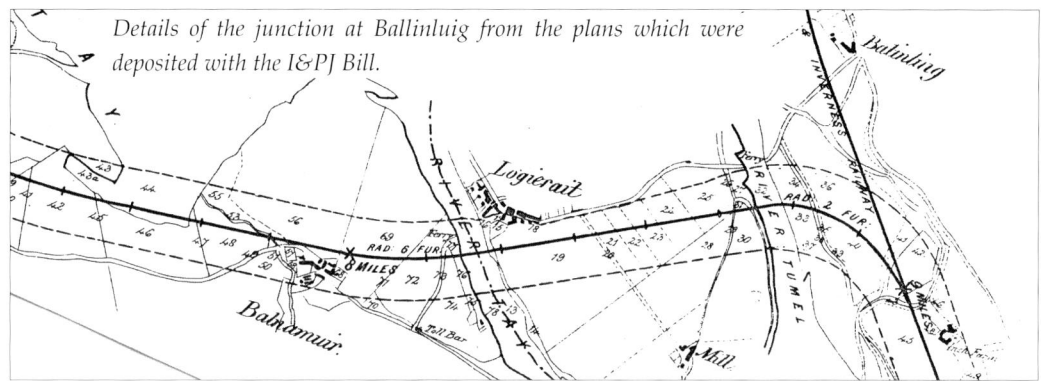

Details of the junction at Ballinluig from the plans which were deposited with the I&PJ Bill.

> For all sugar, grain, corn, flour, hides, dyewoods, earthenware, timber, staves and deals, metals (except iron), nails, anvils, vices, and chains, per ton per mile not exceeding threepence; and if conveyed in carriages belonging to the company, an additional sum per ton per mile not exceeding one penny halfpenny:
>
> For all cotton and other wools, drugs, manufactured goods, and all other wares, merchandise, fish, articles, matters or things, per ton per mile not exceeding fourpence; and if conveyed in carriages belonging to the company, an additional sum per ton per mile not exceeding two pence;
>
> And for every carriage, of whatever description, not being a carriage adapted and used for travelling on a railway, and not weighing more than one ton, carried or conveyed on a truck or platform belonging to the company, per mile not exceeding sixpence; and a further sum of one penny halfpenny per mile for every additional quarter of a ton or fractional part of a quarter of a ton which any such carriage may weigh:
>
> Second, in respect of passengers and animals conveyed in carriages upon the railway, as follows:
>
> For any person conveyed in or upon any such carriage, per mile not exceeding twopence; and if conveyed in or upon any carriages belonging to the company, an additional sum not exceeding one penny per mile:
>
> For every horse, mule, ass or other beasts of draft or burden, and for every ox, cow, bull or meat cattle, conveyed in or upon any such carriage, per mile not exceeding two pence; and if conveyed in or upon any carriage belonging to the company, an additional sum not exceeding threepence per mile:
>
> For every calf, pig, sheep, lamb or other small animal conveyed in or upon such carriage, per mile not exceeding one penny; and if conveyed in or upon any carriage belonging to the company, an additional sum not exceeding one half penny per mile.

Several subsequent clauses relate to limitations and restrictions on the charges for the conveyance of passengers and goods, associated regulations and finally at section 49 the procedures for charging for small parcels and single articles of great weight viz:-

> And with respect to small packages and single articles of great weight, be it enacted, that, notwithstanding the rate of tolls prescribed by this act, the company may lawfully demand tolls not exceeding the tolls following; (that is to say),
>
> For the carriage of small parcels on the railway, as follows:
>
> For any parcel not exceeding seven pounds in weight, fourpence:
>
> For any parcel exceeding seven pounds in weight and not exceeding fourteen pounds in weight, eightpence:
>
> For any parcel exceeding fourteen pounds and not exceeding twenty eight pounds in weight, one shilling:

For any parcel exceeding twenty eight pounds and not exceeding fifty six pounds in weight, one shilling and sixpence:

And for parcels exceeding fifty six pounds in weight, but not exceeding five hundred pounds in weight, the company may demand any sum which they see fit:

Articles sent in large aggregate quantities, although made up of separate parcels, such as bags of sugar, coffee, meal and the like, shall not be deemed small parcels, but such term shall apply only to single parcels in separate packages:

For the carriage of any one boiler, cylinder, or single piece of machinery, or single piece of timber or stone, or other single piece of timber or stone, or other single article, the weight of which including the carriage, shall exceed four tons, but shall not exceed eight tons, the company may demand such sum as they think fit, not exceeding twelve pence per ton per mile:

For the carriage of any single piece of timber, stone, machinery, or other single article, the weight of which, with the carriage, shall exceed eight tons, the company may demand such sum as they see fit.

Despite all the best endeavours unavoidable and unexpected difficulties can and do emerge occasioned by a multitude of factors, such as awkward landowners, financial problems, unforeseen ground conditions and so on, all of which require solutions outwith the terms of the original Act. Or as Robert Burns put it in more succinct terms "The best laid schemes o'Mice and Men gang aft agley". To overcome these problems the Inverness & Perth Junction Railway (Deviations) Act, 1863 was obtained to implement those changes.

Among the various elements of this Act were several sections unique to the Aberfeldy branch. Firstly at Section 8, para vii the Grandtully deviation, the track was re-aligned from a point one mile west of Grandtully and terminating near Lagg. Interestingly the proposed route differed from the original submission in 1846 by passing Grandtully further south away from the River Tay.

Secondly at para viii, the Aberfeldy deviation, commencing at approximately nine hundred yards from the intended terminus in Chapel Street; a diversion southwards was to be constructed ending just south of and parallel to Dunkeld Street, giving an overall reduction of quarter of a mile from the total length of the branch.

There was also a requirement for a road to be constructed between Ballinluig Station and the ferry at the River Tummel, along with a convenient platform at the south side of Ballinluig Station with suitable accommodation for carriages arriving and departing and carts loading and unloading at the said station; all to be at the railway company's expense and maintained in all the time thereafter to the satisfaction of the surveyor for the Strathtay district of turnpike roads.

Lastly a clause detailing compensation was included to compensate owners or occupiers of land which had been entered but was now no longer required.

The Penultimate Hurdle

One would think with all assents, consents and the like confirmed it would be a simple matter to begin the design process and thence appoint a contractor as quickly as practicable. The succeeding extracts from both the minutes of the Inverness & Perth Junction Railway and local newspapers of the period portray a more complicated and convoluted narrative of how the matter was ultimately resolved. To begin with the minute dated 31/1/1862 at paragraph 9 is as follows:-

> Read letter of date the 27th inst. from Sir Robert Menzies in regard to the Aberfeldy branch also letter from the Chairman dated 29th inst. on the same subject from the latter of which it appears that including Lord Breadalbane's subscription the sum of £26,000 has been subscribed in the Aberfeldy district which this board engaged would be sufficient to induce them to proceed with the works of the branch simultaneously with those of the main line. Resolved to express cordial satisfaction that such a large sum has been subscribed in the district – and the Board hope that the balance of subscription may soon be procured. Meanwhile the meeting instructed the engineer to proceed forthwith with preparation of working plans in order to be ready to commence operations when the required subscriptions shall have been made up; and they approved a deputation of directors along with engineer and secretary to meet the subscribers in the Aberfeldy district on Tuesday the 25th day of February next.

Then next month the minute dated 28th February 1862 states:-

> The Chairman reported that a meeting of the inhabitants was held at Aberfeldy on Tuesday 25th at which he attended along with Sir Alexander Cumming and Sir Robert Menzies having stated on behalf of the local committee organised for the purpose of raising subscriptions for the Aberfeldy branch, that they had obtained subscriptions to the amount of £31,000 and that an offer had been made by Sir William Stewart to give his land for the acquisition of the line, which was considered to be the equivalent to a subscription of £2,000, he had replied on behalf of the company that on these conditions being carried out the company would undertake to proceed forthwith with the formation of the Aberfeldy branch. The Chairman also expressed that he had instructed Messrs Inglis and Leslie to let the subscription contract executed for the above amount and to report progress to the Board. The meeting approved and confirmed the undertaking given as above stated by the Chairman and directed the engineer to proceed with the preparation of working plans and sections.

Thereafter in the minute of 10th June 1862 the following was recorded:-

> Read minute of meeting of the committee of the Aberfeldy branch dated June 1 and considering it was a condition of the agreement for carrying on that branch that the proprietors should give their land at valuation, that one of the principal landowners has declined to allow the Company to commence the survey with a view to operating and that another has coupled his consent for this arrangement with compensation, with a condition that should they procure an access through lands belonging to another Company over which they have no control, that this Company have unsuccessfully endeavoured to ensure these obstacles, although it was not part of their agreement to do so.
>
> Resolved that as soon as these difficulties are overcome the Company will proceed forthwith to have the survey made and the matter carried out with due dispatch.

Several months later, indications of problems became manifest as the minute of 23rd April 1863 states:-

Read letter of the 21st inst. from Sir Robert Menzies Bart, in regard to progress being made with the Aberfeldy branch – after consideration it was resolved that Mr McIntosh be requested to explain to Sir Robert when he meets with him this week at Farleyer the reasons which have induced the Board to pause in their operations for the present.

Further confirmation of difficulties came in the following article from *Perthshire Advertiser* of 18th June 1863:-

Aberfeldy – Railway prospects – for upwards of two years we have almost daily been waiting to hear of the Aberfeldy branch of the Inverness and Perth railway, but hitherto we have been disappointed. The ground is again under crop, and it is not likely the directors of the main line will think of incurring the extra expense upon them, were they to cut through the arable ground at this season. From the reports we have from credible authorities, matters do not stand in such a bad position, as most people in the quarter believe; on the contrary, things promise well, once the harvest season is over. Two or three reasons may be given why the branch is left to lie over so long. At present, the directors and contractors of the main line are afraid, that by the month of August the heaviest part of the works of the main line will not be finished, and if they were to commence this branch now, the bulk of the navvies would leave the hills and commence work on the low grounds. We believe, however, the directors have made up their minds to begin the Aberfeldy branch line when the heaviest part of the works of the main line are finished, and they expect to be able to finish it altogether in about eight months. We hear that most of the shareholders in this district, if not the whole of them, are to withdraw their shares, as they took these on the understanding that the works were to be begun immediately, so that some difficulty will be experienced, we fear, in raising funds for the formation of the branch. We only hope that the works shall be begun and soon ended, because a railway to this part of the country could not miss to do a great deal of good – in fact a railway is the only thing it requires – and we have not the slightest doubt, once it was finished and in working order, it will be found to be a well-paying branch.

This standstill in activity caused disquiet amongst shareholders in the area who, desirous of progress, met with procrastination and sophistry from the company. For the company to report that this branch, well below 10% of the total length of venture, could somehow impinge on the construction of the main line is at best questionable. At the time of the article (18th June 1863) the main line was running to Pitlochry and was only a few weeks off completion to Forres; furthermore the railway was constructed sectionally, various contractors undertaking their disparate packages over different parts of the line; to infer labour difficulties, therefore, is tenuous, as I doubt they would ever have materialised. The principal cause of the delay was, I suspect, simply finance; engineering difficulties between Grandtully and Aberfeldy, highlighted earlier in 1846 combined with the required Tummel and Tay crossings, resulted in excessive constructive costs. At the same time the company was facing the financial pressure of completing its main line.

This impasse was, thankfully, brought to its conclusion by the timely and prescient intervention of Sir Robert Menzies, Bart., of Castle Menzies. Sir Robert was, to quote an article in the *Perthshire Advertiser* of 4th July 1928 (on the occasion of the 63rd anniversary of the opening of the line) totally determined and persistent in his efforts to have the line built, the article then goes on to quote Sir Robert Menzies as follows:-

When the Directors declined to proceed with the Aberfeldy branch I cease (sic) to be one, and opposed the amalgamation of the Highland with the Perth and Dunkeld Railway on the grounds no line can amalgamate with another till its whole length had been completed. In that I succeeded and the Perth and Dunkeld Railway was adopted by the Highland with the condition that the directors were to pay a fine of £25 per day to the Queen if the Aberfeldy branch was not completed within the time named. That was done and it has become a good paying bit of the Highland railway even after the two bridges over the Tummel and Tay were imposed on it.

Subsequent minutes now tell a different story as that of 3rd July 1863 shows:

Resolved to advertise the works of the Aberfeldy branch in time for tenders being considered on the 1st September.

And that of 24th day of September is as follows:-

Resolved to advertise for offers for the work of the Aberfeldy branch as soon as plans are ready.

Also from 13th day of October 1863:-

Read letter of date of the 10th inst. from Messrs H&A Inglis W.S. stating that Sir William Stewart requires £4,000 to be consigned in the bank before he gives possession of his land for commencing the works of the Aberfeldy branch. Resolved to authorise to agent to consign the money accordingly.

The newspapers too confirm this change as the *Perthshire Advertiser* of November 26th 1863 reported:-

Aberfeldy – our branch railway – contractors are now going over the ground, with a view of lodging their tenders for the works of this branch. Trial pits are being opened here and there, as far as they have gone, we understand everything turns out well and is progressing favourably, so in time we may expect to hear of arrangements being made for cutting the first turf by the 1st of January.

The same newspaper of 17th December 1863 wrote the following:-

Aberfeldy – Railway – We understand preparations are now being made for commencing our branch line of railway as soon as possible. The trial pits, which we formerly noticed as having been begun, are now approaching completion, and so far everything appears to be going favourably. On Tuesday, the 8th instant, nine or ten of the railway contractors were going over the line, with the view of making out

At Ballinluig, the branch platform was tacked on to that on the main line which can be seen in the distance. The branch leads off in the left foreground to the Tummel viaduct. (David Stirling)

and lodging tenders for the works. The soil being chiefly gravel, and a mixture of hard clay and sand, the only great difficulty connected with it will be the procuring of stones for the overway and underway bridges, of which it seems there will be thirty-five, besides the two viaducts across the Tummel and the Tay. This want, however, can be easily supplied from quarries in this district and neighbourhood, although the company will, of course, be put to a little more expense. For some time a doubt existed as to what part of the village the station, or rather the terminus, was to be in; but we believe the directors have at last come to the conclusion to have it at the extreme end, and it will in this way save a good deal of money; although for the good of the village, we have no doubt it would be better to have it close to the square, where they first thought of having it. We may say, we still think the branch will turn out to be one of the best paying parts of the line.

As the preceding newspaper reports state, the tendering process was nearing its conclusion, the various contractors now having lodged their offers with the company. A contract would be concluded with the issue of an acceptance; the ensuing two minutes, are therefore, the most vital to date, initiating the certain construction process. Firstly from the meeting of 29th December 1863 at para 3:-

The following tenders for the works of the Aberfeldy branch together with a report by the engineer on the same were laid on the table viz:

1.	Messrs Gorrans and Mackay	£ 69517.10.11
2.	Mr Alexander Wilson, Granton	69191. 0. 0
3.	Mr John Grainger, Tain	67234.12. 1
4.	Messrs Prudham	64220. 7. 8
5.	Messrs Charles Brand & Sons. Fordoun	61817.18. 8
6.	Mr James McNaughton, Ayr	61000. 0. 0
7.	Messrs McDonald & Grieve	60989. 3. 5

After discussion it was resolved to accept the offer of Messrs McDonald and Grieve, provided they settle with the engineer for their extra claims on the Invergordon and Dalnacardoch contract and failing a satisfactory arrangement of these the offer of Brand and Sons be accepted.

Secondly from the meeting of 25th day of January 1864 also at para 3:-

The tenders received for the permanent way materials required for the Aberfeldy branch line were laid on the table together with a report thereon by the engineers. After discussion it was resolved to accept the following viz:-

Messrs Guest & Co, London	For rails	£ 8.18 / -	per ton
	For fish plates	10.10 / -	per ton
	For bolts	19.15 / -	per ton
John Whitelaw, Dunfermline	For chairs	4.12 / 6	per ton
Alex Livingston, Aberfeldy	For 10,125 larch sleepers	2 /10½	each
Peter McAinsh, Granton	For 10,125 larch sleepers	3 / -	each

A legally binding commitment was now in place to build the Aberfeldy branch, the genesis of a new age now evolving and the local area both expectant and euphoric regarding its future as the *Perthshire Advertiser* reported on the turf cutting ceremony of Jan 21st 1864:-

Aberfeldy – The railway – The dawn of the day of prosperity has at last gleamed upon Aberfeldy, which has long been looked upon as the capital of the Perthshire Highlands; but it did not bear that name with as much truthfulness in the past as undoubtedly it will do in the future. Several articles relative to our branch railway have now for many months appeared in our columns, and in many of these we have expressed our anxious hope that the commencement of the works would not long be delayed. At last, and all of a sudden, our wishes are fully satisfied. On Monday last, the 18th instant, which was fixed for the cutting of the first turf, an immense crowd of old and young crowded our streets, both of the people of the town, gentry, and strangers, from the surrounding districts, who at one o'clock in the afternoon, headed by a piper, marched off to the east end of the village, eager to witness the performance of the ceremony. After a suitable prayer had been offered up by the Rev. Mr Clarke, Aberfeldy, the honourable Mrs Menzies of Chesthill, who, accompanied by Chesthill her very worthy husband had that morning, although bitterly cold, driven into the town to honour us with their presence on this special occasion began her work of cutting the turf and filling the barrow in a most systematic and manly way. After having performed this work, twice filling and twice emptying the barrow, a vote of thanks to the Hon. Lady moved by Mr Wyllie, Bolfracks, was most heartily joined in by the crowd of spectators by loud and long continuous cheering. In returning thanks for his lady, Chesthill stated, that he had much pleasure in being present on this occasion, and that he had to thank them all for the cordial manner in which they had to joined in the vote of thanks by Mr Wyllie, and said he had no doubt a lady standing beside him would have performed the ceremony in a much better manner, and was in every way much better fitted for it, upon which Mrs Menzies was observed to eye the lady from head to foot and looked at her as is she would like to think "I'm not so sure about that?" Every one present then joined in three cheers to the directors and contractors of the line, the crowd dispersed. The barrow used on this occasion was a handsome one, made of mahogany, and presented by Mr Duncan Ritchie, cabinet maker, Aberfeldy. The spade was of polished steel with mahogany handle, and was presented by Mr Stewart, Saddler, Aberfeldy. The Hon. Mrs Menzies was asked to accept both barrow and spade as a memento of the auspicious event. At three o'clock a number of the merchants and others interested in the prosperity of the town, retired to the Breadalbane Arms hotel where they sat down to a sumptuous dinner, prepared for them by Mr McKenzie. Mr Wyllie occupied the chair, supported on the right and left by the Rev. Mr Clarke, Dr Reid, Aberfeldy, Mr Grieve, Railway Contractor, and Rev Mr McLean, Grandtully. Mr Forbes, Solicitor acted as croupier supported by Lieutenant Craigie, Strathtay, and Mr Wyllie junior, Bolfracks. Dinner over, and the "succeeding port" having been placed on the table, the following toasts were given:- The Queen, The Prince and The Princess of Wales, Army, Navy and volunteers, and the Lord of the manor, the Earl of Breadalbane by the chairman, the last of which was drunk with Highland honours. The clergy, by Mr Paterson, success to the railway, by the chairman. The chairman and directors of the company, by the croupier, who noticing the death of his grace the Duke of Athole one of the directors expressed a wish that this toast be drunk without cheering which was accordingly done. The contractors – Messrs McDonald and Grieve by the Rev. Mr Clarke. The Hon Mrs Menzies of Chesthill by Mr Wyllie junior, Chesthill by Mr Lauchlan McLean, Pitilie, which after a humorous and very able speech by Mr McLean was drunk with highland honours. The trade and prosperity of Aberfeldy, by Lieutenant Craigie. In consequence of the Duke of Athole's death, numbers were prevented from attending who would have otherwise been present. It was much regretted that Chesthill was not present at the dinner; but having some business to do, and a long journey before him, he was obliged to go away. As the turf is now cut, we have no doubt the contractors will do their utmost to have the works pushed on with all possible speed and we hope that within fifteen months, at furthest, we will have the present duty of reporting that the works are finished, and the line open for traffic.

Eloquent, wordy or loquacious may aptly describe the foregoing feature; it was, however, of its time and also descriptive of events of that time. Some explanation is perhaps required to clarify the phrase "Highland honours" when applied to certain toasts; it refers to a toast given while standing on your chair, having one foot on the table. Douce, dour or Presbyterian would, therefore, not correctly describe demeanour on the day. I doubt that would concern those present; the railway was at last coming to Aberfeldy and thus worthy of great celebration!

20   *Aberfeldy's Railway*

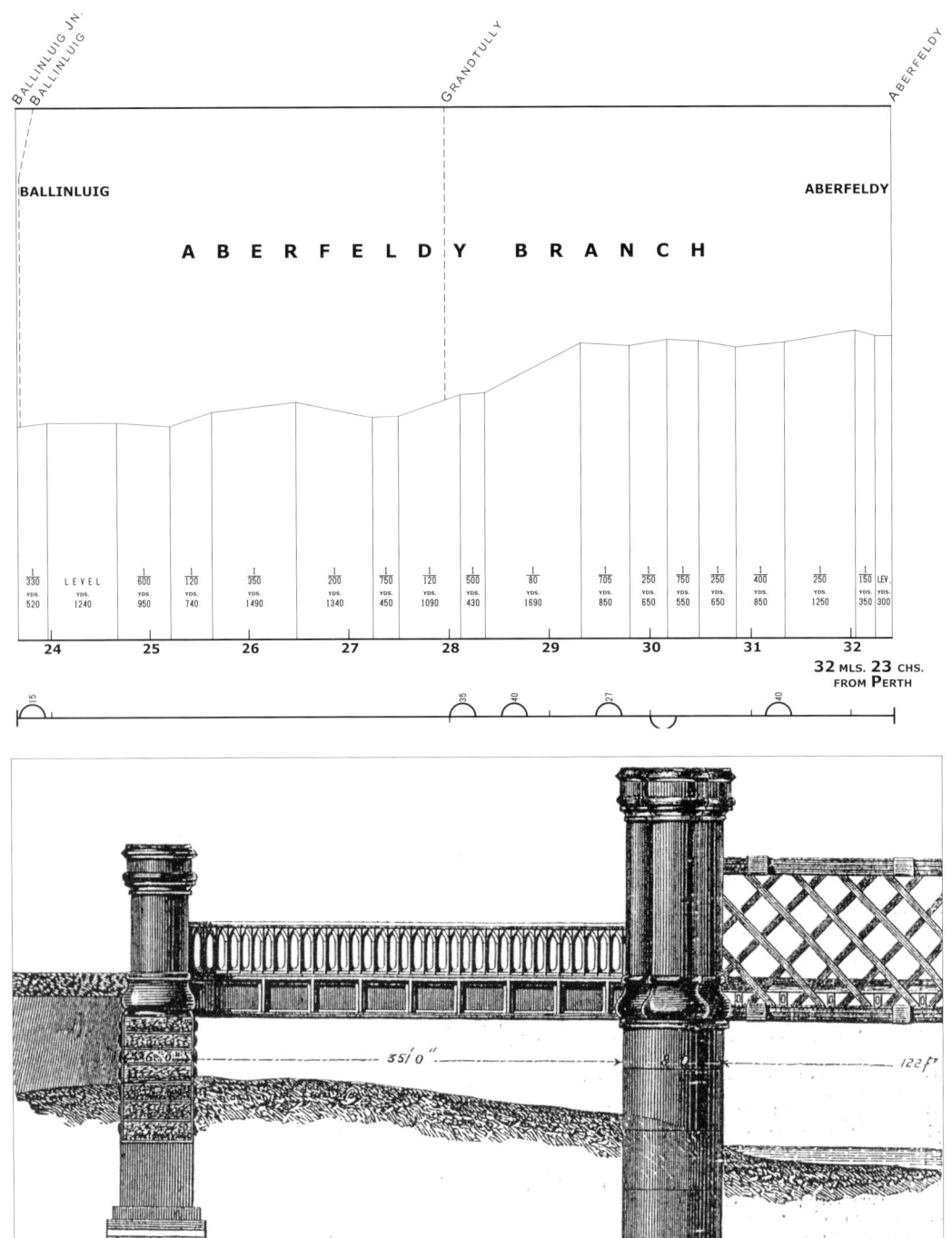

Abutment of Tummel Viaduct from 'Engineering'. In 1867, this publication carried a detailed description of the various bridges and viaducts designed by Joseph Mitchell for the Highland Railway which included this illustration.

Constructing the Line

When the contractors first surveyed the route of the line they would have been confronted with a landscape and topography that typifies much of Highland Scotland, the glorious fusion of hills, glens and rivers that moulds our wonderful scenery. Commencing at Ballinluig the line heads westwards, crossing in its first mile both the Tummel and Tay, continuing thereafter across the broad valley floor that is Strathtay past Logierait and Balnaguard to Grandtully. This section apart from the two major river crossings was relatively straightforward; a few cuttings and embankments were required but nothing exceptional or untoward was encountered. From Grandtully to Aberfeldy was, however, a different proposition; the landscape changes from flat strath to a narrow steep sided defile formed between Grandtully Hill in the south and Farragon and its outliers to the north, the Tay twisting and turning through it. This section not surprisingly necessitated extensive earth-moving and considerable bridgeworks to negotiate a route to its final destination in Aberfeldy. Luckily, however, some of the problems frequently met whilst working in the Highlands were avoided, neither rock nor peat were experienced thus obviating the necessity to blast, tunnel or float the line. Nevertheless this branch was in cost per mile the most expensive built by the company, due principally to two factors, the Tummel and Tay crossings and the aforementioned extensive earthworks required between Grandtully and Aberfeldy.

The River Tay is Scotland's longest river, carrying a greater volume of water than all the other major rivers combined. Its headwaters originate on Ben Lui near Tyndrum, and it flows eastwards through Strath Fillan, Glen Dochart and Loch Tay, with added flow coming from the rivers Lochy, Lyon and countless burns. The Tummel, too, is a significant river, originating in far off Rannoch Moor at Lochs Ba and Laidon, thence running through Lochs Rannoch and Tummel with major tributaries such as the Garry and Tilt feeding down from Druimuachdhar. The enormous combined watershed, extending to the boundaries that Perthshire has with the counties of Argyll and Inverness, creates an area subject to considerable rainfall and snowfall which, consequently, can lead to severe flooding downstream particularly where the relatively flat strath creates a natural floodplain that can dissipate this excess flow. The Tummel and Tay were, therefore the major obstacles to be overcome, but overcome they were using new and innovative methods in their construction as the following paper given by Joseph Mitchell FRSE, FGS, CE, and read before the British Association in September 1869 explains. (Bridge No1 is omitted from this extract, it being the Tay bridge at Dalguise carrying the main line)

> Numbers 2 and 3 are the most recent bridges erected by the writer and here he has taken advantage of the modern plan of using cylinder piers to carry girders. Both bridges are constructed in the same manner, and the same principle. The cylinders form the piers in the centre and abutments. Each cylinder is 8 feet in diameter, and was sunk into the bed of the river 27½ feet in their extreme depth, by means of divers. When these cylinders were adjusted and brought to the full depth, about three feet of cement concrete was lowered into the bottom. On the concrete setting, the water was pumped out, and the interior filled with rubble masonry, laid with Portland cement. To provide for extreme floods two side openings were made 41½ and 45 feet span, of plate girders, one end resting on the masonry in the cast iron cylinders and the other on a stone abutment landward, secured on a platform and piles. These bridges answer their purpose very satisfactorily.

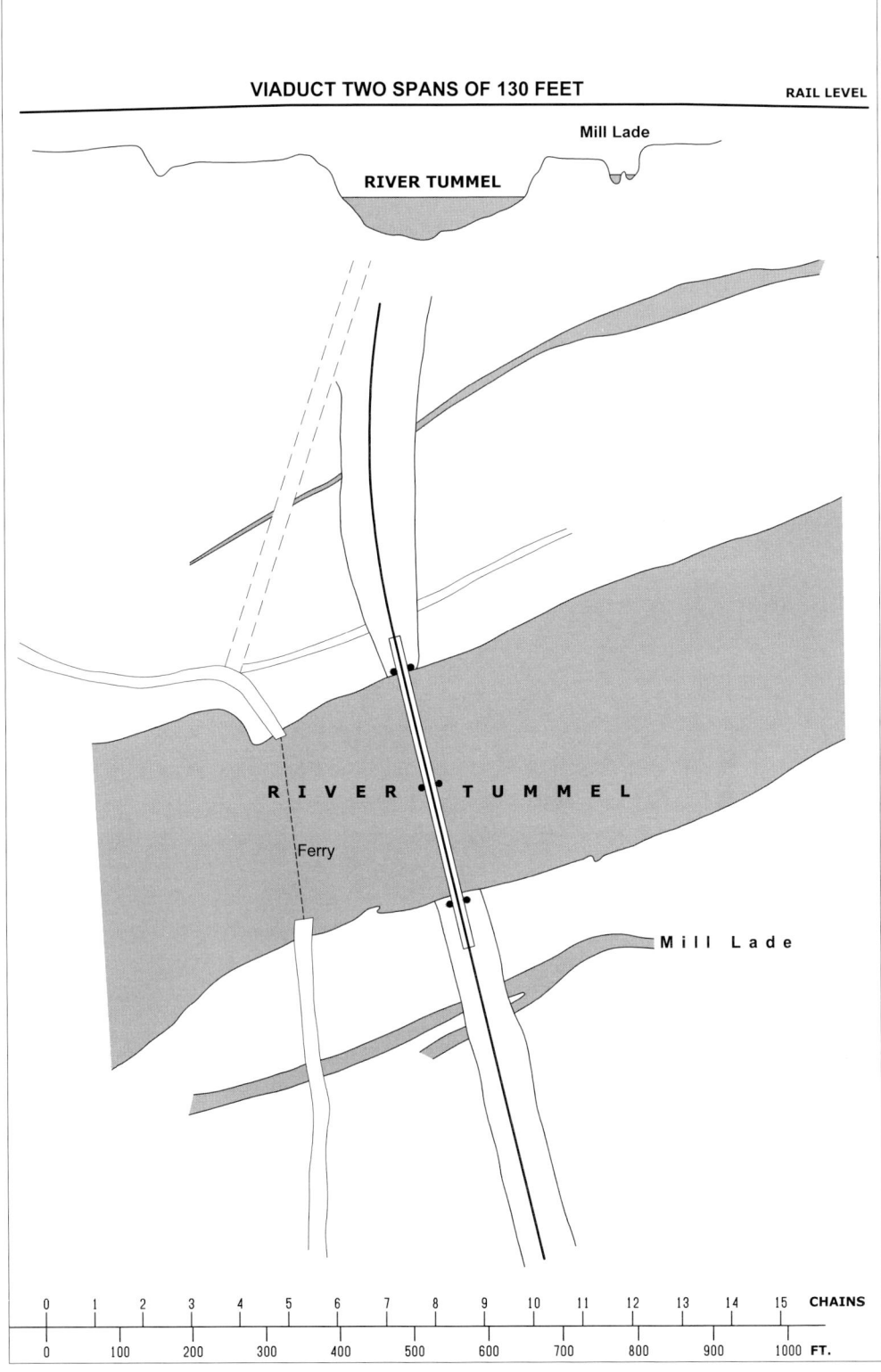

River Tummel Viaduct from the plans for the branch, c1863.

Constructing the Line

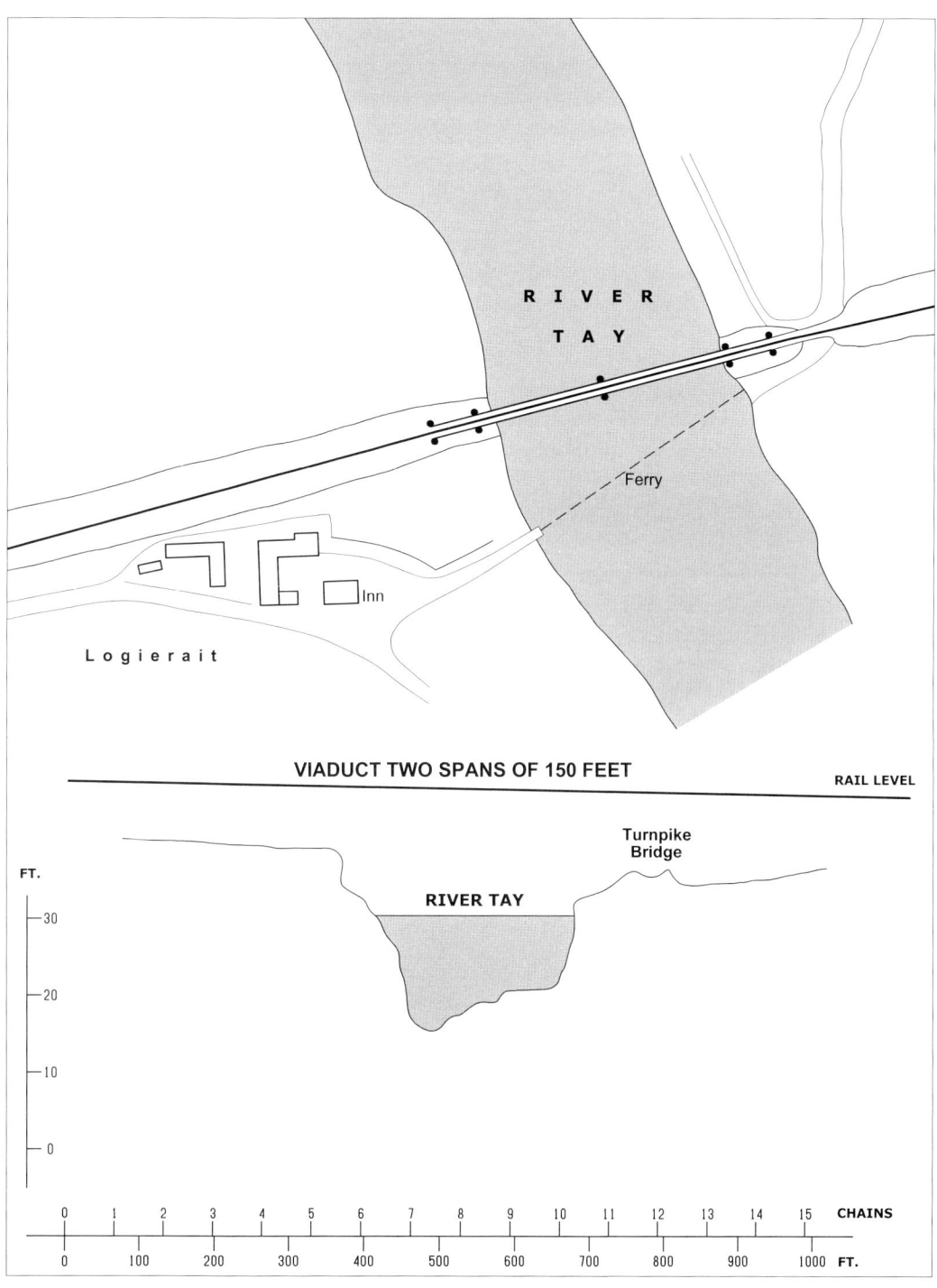

River Tay Viaduct from the plans for the branch, c1863.

The cost of No. 2 bridge, which consists of two openings of 122 feet and two side openings of 35 feet span was £11,156. The total length of No.2, 350 feet; cost per linear foot £31/17/6; height above bed of river 36 feet.

The cost of No.3 bridge consisting of two openings of 137 feet and two side openings of 41½ feet span, the cylinders being sunk into the bed of the river 25 feet, amounted to £13,770, length of No. 3 419½ feet, cost £32/16/7 per linear foot, height above bed of river 49 feet.

These bridges were built by Messrs Fairbairn and Co, Manchester under the supervision of Mr Passmore C.E. and after completion were tested, using as reported in the *Perthshire Advertiser*:-

the weight of the four heaviest engines on the line, and, the utmost deflection was only, in the case of the Tummel Bridge, ⅝ and 1-16th of an inch [$^{11}/_{16}$ ths] and in the case of the Tay bridge, ⅝ths of an inch.

This result was regarded as very satisfactory. The total expenditure on these two structures was £24,926 which contributed nearly £2,950 to the cost per mile of the branch, a considerable amount when compared with the figure of approximately £200 per mile of the bridge at Dalguise being spread over the entire 100 mile of the main line.

The second factor in cost was the large scale earthworks required to bring the route through the defile between Grandtully and Aberfeldy. Grandtully Hill at 1747 feet commands the southern flank, sloping at an average 1 in 10 northwards to the river over a distance of nearly four miles. It was these slopes the line had to traverse, not in itself technically difficult as in normal circumstances a shelf could be excavated to accommodate the line. This was, however, not possible on Grandtully Hill as its gravel based sub-soil had, over the centuries, been the subject of fluvial erosion forming countless gullies which dissected its flanks creating a switchback effect. When examined in cross section it is seen as constantly varying, and from the proposed rail level has vertical differences above and below of up to 50 feet. Extensive cut and fill was therefore required in this section, along with the associated bridging at roads, burns and the like.

From an examination of the original engineering sections it can be found that the total cut/fill quantities were 782,430 cubic yards; these drawings also show subsequent amended quantities. Notwithstanding those later changes this quantity on an 8¾ mile long railway is massive but even

Tummel Viaduct as built in 1864 by Macdonald & Grieve/Fairbairn Engineering Co, contractors. It consisted of two spans of 122 feet with side openings 35 feet. (HRS Roberts collection)

Tay Viaduct as built by Macdonald & Grieve/Fairbairn Engineering Co. It consisted of two spans of 137 feet and side openings of 41½ feet. (HRS Roberts collection)

more pertinent are the various splits. Excavation totalled 421,780 and filling 360,650 cubic yards; this equates to a typical cross section cut/fill average of approximately 50 cubic yards per yard of line. In reality, however, it meant that Ballinluig to Grandtully would be nearer 30 whereas Grandtully to Aberfeldy more likely 70 cubic yards, that is an average 25 x 25 foot cross section, roughly the size of a gable of a two storey house in area!

Those conditions also called for considerable bridges to span the many burns and tracks in the area, both over and under. Various numbers are bandied about and I cannot be totally conclusive on this matter, suffice to say that the original archive shows two viaducts (Tummel and Tay), twenty two bridges, nine culverts and seven cattle creeps, forty in total; the inventory of fixed assets at closure lists a total of forty two, an average of nearly five per mile. Similarly the ratio per mile between Grandtully and Aberfeldy would be higher, probably nearer seven per mile.

Despite those difficult conditions encountered work progressed steadily, excavating, bridge building, track preparation and so on moving inexorably towards completion. The contractor, it was

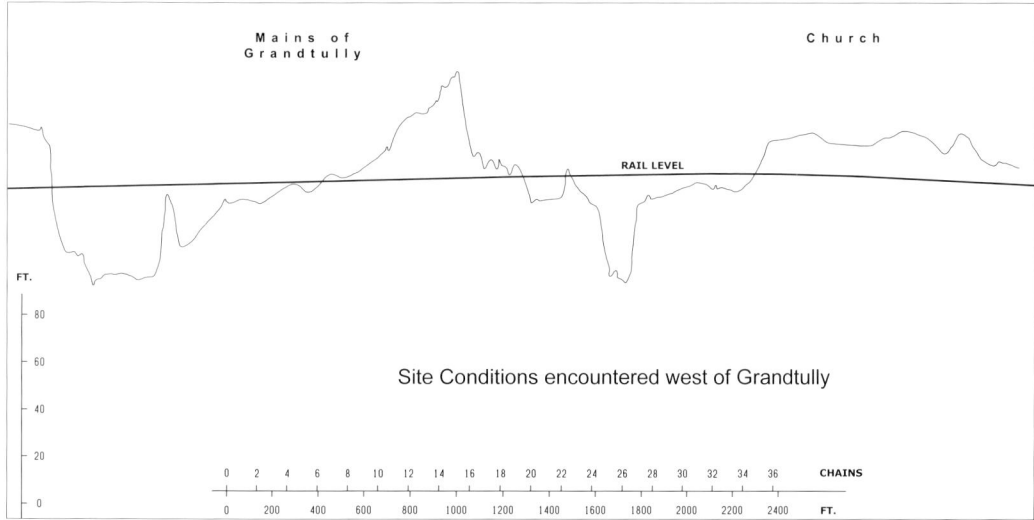

reported, had good industrial relations with his force of navvies; records and reports indicate he rewarded his men after the completion of major cuttings with a fair amount of whisky. The local newspapers, too, paid an active interest in progress as the *Perthshire Courier* of 21st March 1865 reported:-

> BALNAGUARD – THE RAILWAY – *The Tummel viaduct is now proceeding at rapid pace towards a finish. The fitters and rivetters are actively involved on the ironwork, and in some short time we may expect to see the same at Tay Viaduct, as the pillars and abutments are almost ready.*

Even during the construction process some matters had yet to be finalised, especially the location of the stations. This was ultimately decided upon as the Company minutes of 19th May 1864 show:-

> *The Chairman reported that he visited the works of the Aberfeldy branch and found that satisfactory progress was being made. He brought under consideration of the meeting the sites proposed for stations, three in number. After examining the plans the meeting was of the opinion that the sites proposed should be abandoned, and in lieu thereof a station be erected at Grandtully and a platform for passengers at Lagg.*

It would appear that the platform was constructed but no buildings were ever constructed. The importance of Lagg seems to have been determined by its nearness to Grandtully distillery, the Cluny ferry and Killiechassie.

The stations at Grandtully and the Aberfeldy terminus were, nonetheless, constructed, Grandtully possessing a platform, loading bank, sidings, station building, stores, latrine, coal shed and crane; that at Aberfeldy comprising platform, loading banks, sidings, station building, latrines/stores, water tower, engine shed and crane. Associated and requisite telegraph and signalling equipment was also installed along the line. Finally the project was complete, only one last hurdle to be overcome, the official inspection. The *Perthshire Courier* of 4th July 1865 describes this and the events of this momentous day as follows:-

Thomas A Fyfe, station master at Aberfeldy from the opening until 1902, was held in high regard.

> *The Aberfeldy railway was inspected on Saturday by the government inspector Captain Rich C.E., he was accompanied by Aeneas McIntosh Esq of Raigmore; Cluny McPherson, Esq; Major Cummings Bruce, M.P.; Mr Andrew Dougall, Inverness; Mr Joseph Mitchell, C.E.; Mr Murdoch Paterson, C.E., Inverness; Mr Buttle, General Manager, permanent way; Mr D Jones, locomotive department; Messrs Fyfe, Lamont and Bulmer; Mr Anderson, Solicitor, Inverness; Mr Passmore, Superintendent of bridges; Mr E.O. Douglas, Killiechassie; Colonel Murray, Moness; Mr Wylie, Bolfracks; Mr H.R.B. Piell, factor to Sir R Menzies; Mr George Rankin, Banker, Aberfeldy; Col Dewar, Pitlochry; Mr Oswald, Dunniker; Mr P.S. Kerr, Kindrogan; Mr John Kirk W.S., Edinburgh; and Captain Craigie, Tomandroighne.*
>
> *The inspection was highly satisfactory. The two lattice girder bridges were tested with the weight of the four heaviest engines of the line. Having now been sanctioned by the government inspector, the line was opened for general traffic yesterday.*

After the inspection the company dined in the Breadalbane arms at Aberfeldy. Major Bruce presided, and a large party was present. A number of them had to leave in the course of a very short time in order to enable them to return home by the evening trains, but a goodly party remained. After dinner, the chairman gave the usual loyal and patriotic toast, which was cordially responded to. He thereafter gave "success to the Aberfeldy branch", which was also most enthusiastically received. The chairman then gave the health of Captain Rich, which was duly honoured. Captain Rich replied. Sir Robert Menzies gave the health of the directors of the Inverness and Perth railway, which was acknowledged by the Chairman, who thereafter gave the Lord of the Manor, the Earl of Breadalbane, followed by the health of the neighbouring proprietors, the latter being acknowledged by Sir Robert Menzies.

Captain Rich having signified approval of the line, several trains ran over it on Saturday evening, and it will be formally opened for traffic today. There will be four trains run daily from each end of the line, which will be amply sufficient for the accommodation of the traffic in the district. There is only one intermediate station on the line, that at Grandtully; but it is anticipated that another will by and by be set down at Boat of Lagg to meet the requirement of the district. Mr Fyfe (late of Perth) has been appointed Manager at Aberfeldy; and, from his energetic business habits, we have no doubt nothing will be wanting on his part to develop the traffic of the county.

Nearly twenty years had elapsed since those first dreams, with much frustration, disillusionment and even despair along the way. However, thanks to the local pressure the oft dashed hopes became reality; Aberfeldy had a railway and was now in direct communication with railway network. It is perhaps interesting to look at, albeit in some elements as an educated guess, the final cost of the branch:-

Construction Costs
Initial contract with McDonald and Grieve	£ 60,989
Additional monies approved by Highland Railway Co in September 1866	9,100
Tummel and Tay viaducts	24,926
Rails, fishplates, bolts etc	13,000
Sleepers	3,000
	£ 111,015

Land Acquisition Costs
Duke of Athole	2,929
Sir William Stewart	4,273
Lord Breadalbane	2,450
Payment to tenants (allowance)	1,000
	£ 10,652
Total	£ 121,667

Construction costs alone give a cost per mile of nearly £12,700 and with acquisition costs added this rises to £13,900. An expensive branch indeed when compared with the reported £8,000 per mile of the main line. Consider, however, the assertion of Sir Robert Menzies who argued that this branch was not to be looked at in isolation but as an integral part of the whole and then reflect on the following:

Main line (100 miles say) at 8,000 per mile	£ 800,000
Aberfeldy branch, 8¾ miles	121,667
	£ 921,667

The average cost per mile for the whole undertaking is now £8,475; the expression lies, damned lies and statistics is somehow brought to mind.

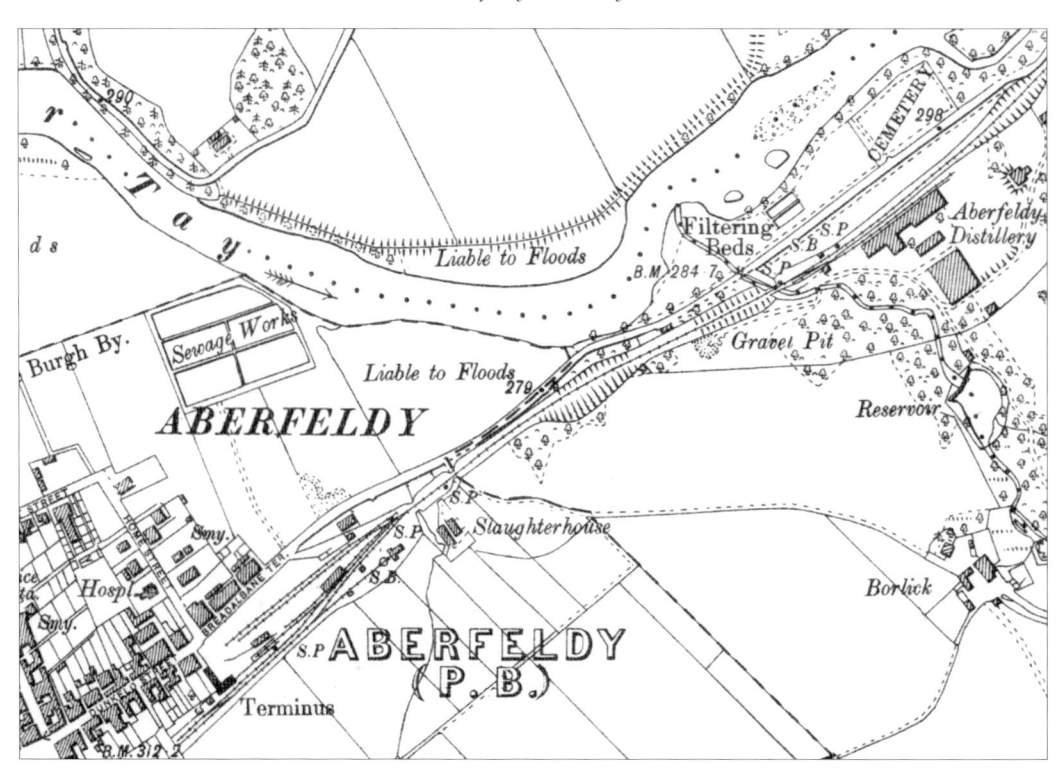

Aberfeldy and Ballinluig as shown on the Ordnance Survey 6 inch map of 1900, although the track layout would have been surveyed some years earlier. *(Reproduced by permission of the National Library of Scotland)*

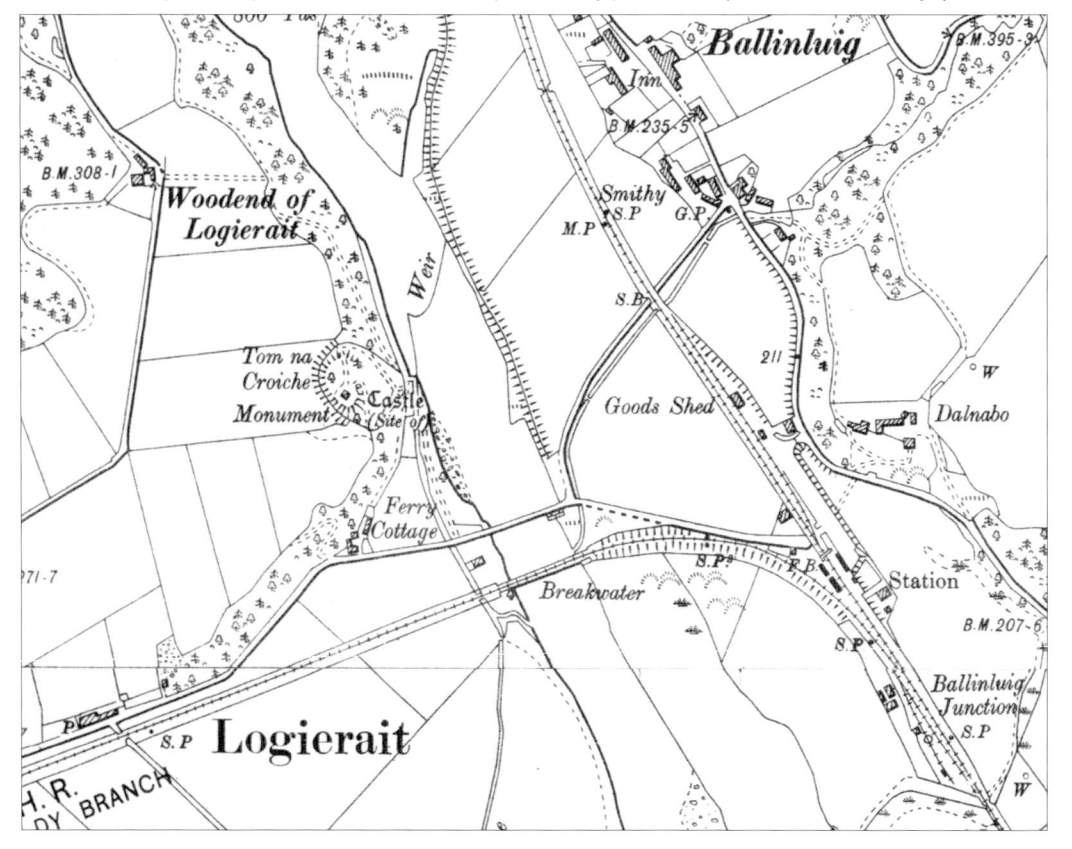

Initial Impact

As previously stated the Strathtay area was a land based economy, the land being in the hands of a few aristocrats or gentry, some even in these Victorian times absentee and managed by factors, with numerous lessees and tenants. Rents and feus are the principal source of income for these estates. Land which was compulsorily acquired had to be paid for, rents adjusted and damage sustained by severance or disturbance had to be recompensed. The following data obtained from the twenty page Book of Reference relating to the Aberfeldy branch gives a clear indication of the extent of properties involved.

Firstly was the parish of Logierait which extends from Ballinluig to the River Tay. This parish was in the entire ownership of the Duke of Athole, except for the Strathtay Turnpike road. It contained seventy three properties, had three lessees and eleven occupiers. Secondly was the parish of Little Dunkeld which lies to the west of the Tay to midway between Balnaguard and Haugh of Grandtully, three miles one furlong from Ballinluig; it was owned by the Duke of Athole, Sir William Drummond Stewart, Baronet, and the Strathtay and Bishopric turnpikes, and comprised seventy one properties, with eight lessees and sixteen occupiers. Thirdly in the list of parishes is Dull which continues from the boundary of Little Dunkeld to the end of the line with a three furlong segment removed for the parish of Weem. The landowners in Dull were Sir William Drummond Stewart, Baronet, the Marquess of Breadalbane and the Bishopric turnpike; it was made up of two hundred and sixty three properties, having thirty lessees and sixty one occupiers. Lastly is the parish of Weem, bounded on both sides by Dull, beginning at just over eight miles from Ballinluig and extending westwards for approximately three furlongs. All in the ownership of the Marquess of Breadalbane, it comprised twenty seven properties and had three lessees and six occupiers.

From the above it will be appreciated that considerable numbers of lessees and occupiers existed with a lesser number of owners, all of whom received payments for ground acquired whether owner or tenant. From the archives in Blair Castle a picture emerges of how these matters were dealt with:

List of tenants of the Duke of Athole who have signed agreements with the Inverness and Perth junction railway (Aberfeldy branch) and where shown the respective annual payments agreed in a subsequent conveyance between the Duke of Athole and the Highland railway company – for and on account value of land taken and damage by severance to their respective farms

Mrs Elizabeth McGregor	Ballinluig	£ 5 / 11 /-
Neil Stewart	Dalnab	£ 7 / 5 / 5
David Reid	Inch of Dalnab	£ 2 / -
James Stewart	Tummel Ferry	£ 4 / 12 /-
Duncan Robertson	Easter Logierait	
James McLeish	Port of Logierait	£ 1 / 6
James Campbell	Dalnamuir	£ 5 / 6 / -
Robert Butter	Dalnair	£ 3 / 18 /-
John and Duncan Campbell	Craiganuisk	£ 7 / 13 / 8
James Menzies	Balnaguard	£ 8 / 10 / 6
Donald McDonald	Balnaguard	£ 8 / 8 / -
Margaret Forbes (Crofter)	"	£ 2 / 4 / -

Mungo Conacher (Crofter)	Balnaguard	£ 1 / 18 / -
James McDonald (")	"	£ 2 / - / -
James McGregor (")	"	£ 1 / 2 / -
John McLaren (")	"	£ 2 / 6 / -
Margaret Helen and Susan Jamieson	Logierait Ferry	£ 6 / 12 / -
Mrs Catherine Duff	Mill of Logierait	[No figure quoted]

Similar principles were involved in making payments to landowners, not surprisingly the sums are somewhat greater as this archive record shows:-

Statement of Settlement between his Grace the Duke of Athole and the Highland Railway Company for land taken for the Aberfeldy branch

3rd Nov 1868

1. Value of 17.2.34 (acres/roods/poles) of land taken   £ 1584. 1. 1
   Severance damage   562. 10. 0
   Sum to be consigned with interest from Whitsy [Whit Sunday] 1864   £ 2146. 11. 1
2. Sums allowed for diverting Ballinluig water into
   Tummel with interest from Whitsy   £ 100.
3. Sums allowed for value of earth with interest
   from Whitsy 1866   £ 180.   280. 0. 0
   £ 2426. 11. 1

Interest on above sums to 10th September 1868 when the amount was deposited in bank at 5 per cent less income tax as follows
   On No 1 £2146.11.1 from Whitsy 1864   453. 11. 12
   2 £100   "   "   1866   16. 6. 0
   3 £180   "   "   1866   20. 9. 10   490. 7. 0
   Total at September 1868   £2916. 18. 1
   Add interest on this sum at 2 per cent   12. 18. 11
   Total due   £2929. 17. 0

Edinburgh 30th November 1868 received by us as agents of His Grace The Duke of Athole from the Highland Railway Company by the hands of Messrs H&A Inglis W.S. the above sum of Two thousand, nine hundred and twenty nine pounds, seventeen shillings, the conveyance by his in favour of the Company having been at the same time handed to Messrs Inglis; and we undertake to consign the above sum of £2929.17.0 in the Bank of Scotland in terms of the Land Clauses Consolidation (Scotland) Act of 1845.

It is interesting to note that all these figures were arrived at independently by the arbiter, Robert Elliot, Dunkeld. The sum of £180 at No.3 was a combination of three separate components, £120 being allowed for the value of earth/gravel and other material taken from the site cutting at Logierait, £50 for rock taken by the contractor for various building works, and thirdly £10 to enable the installation of a pump on the farm at Balnamuir to supply water to a field deprived of same by the formation of the railway. Although the Duke of Athole through his agents contested some of the figures, they did, however, remain unchanged.

Finally, in this section, I will relate this intriguing little tale of the repercussions after the construction of the Tummel and Tay viaducts, best described as unintended consequences. It began with a Mr John Robertson, Old Blair, Blair Athole writing to His Grace to complain that the tenants of both Tay and Tummel ferries have lodged repeated complaints against the railway company for allowing the viaduct stagings to be used by the public as thoroughfares thus seriously damaging ferry revenues. This in turn was transmitted to the agents of the Duke of Athole and thence to the Board of Trade in London who duly wrote about these concerns to the railway company. The response of the Highland Railway was as follows:-

The Highland Railway Company
General Managers Secretary's Office
Inverness
18 April 1867

The Assistant Secretary
Railway Department Board of Trade
London S.W.
Sir
Ref 655

I have to acknowledge the receipt of your letter dated 6th instant in transmitting copy of a letter from your agents calling attention to the dangers incurred by the public in consequence of foot passengers passing over the railway bridges at the rivers Tay and Tummel, near Logierait.

I am requested by the Directors to state in reply that the bridges referred to are in close proximity to the Ballinluig station where the Aberfeldy branch of the Highland railway forms a junction with the main line. In these circumstances it is most difficult to prevent passengers crossing in the manner complained of. The Company's officials have strict orders to prevent them so crossing and the directors believe they do all in their power to put a stop to it.

I am requested further to state that the company will gladly co-operate with your agents in prosecuting two or three cases which may have a beneficial effect.

I am. etc
Andrew Dougall
Secretary

The Board of Trade in London would now have found out, or perhaps had a re-affirmation, of the well known Scottish saying that "you cannae tak the breeks off a heilan man" as a consequence of that last paragraph.

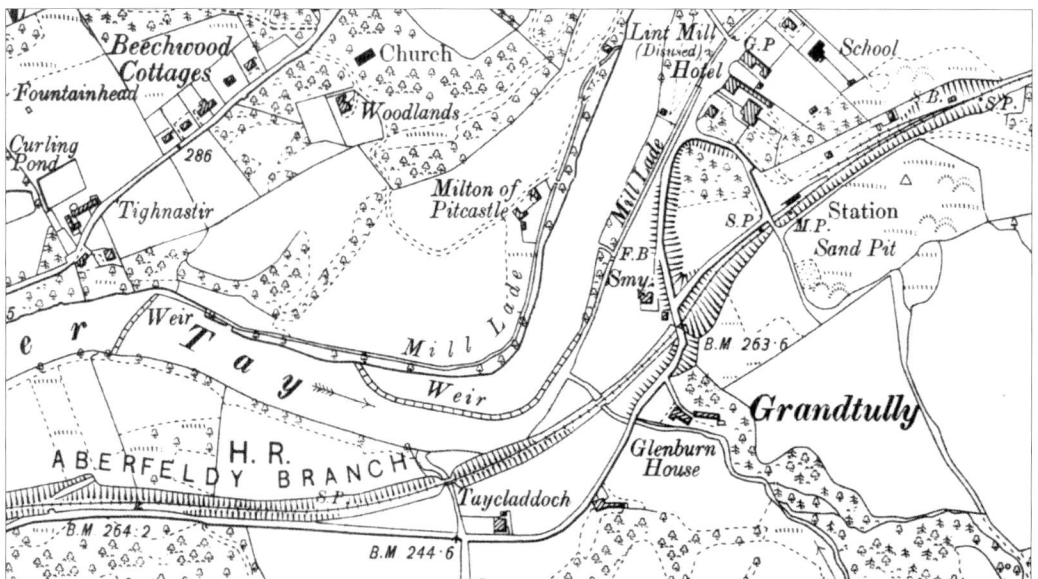

OS 6 inch map of Grandtully, not to scale. (Reproduced by permission of the National Library of Scotland)

Circular Tour No 14

Loch Earn and Loch Tay

By Rail to Crieff; by coach Crieff to Lochearnhead; by rail to Killin; by coach Killin to Aberfeldy; thence by rail to destination.

Tickets available for one month, with liberty to break journey at any of the stations or places on the route.

Examples. Fares for the round, included coachman's fees.

		1st Class	3rd Class
From	Glasgow	64 / 3	38 / 9
	Perth	22 / 9	18 / 3

Circular Tour No 16

Loch Lomond, Glenfalloch, Killin, Loch Tay, Kenmore, Taymouth, Aberfeldy, Perth.

Tickets, available for fourteen days, are issued at Edinburgh and Glasgow (Queen Street) for the tour to Balloch Pier by rail, Balloch Pier to head of Loch Lomond by steamer, hence by coach to Crianlarich, Crianlarich to Killin by rail, Killin to Aberfeldy by coach, thence to destination via Perth; or the route may be reversed.

Fares including coachman's fees

Edinburgh (Waverley and Haymarket)	42 / 6
Glasgow (Queen Street)	37 / 6

Passengers may break the journey at any station on the route, but only at Tarbet and Inversnaid on Loch Lomond.

Running alongside the River Tay. (HRS collection)

Changes and Benefits

Now that it had a railway connection, the area experienced considerable changes to both its social fabric and economic well being; these fell into three main categories; the movement of people, the growth of tourism and associated leisure activities and lastly the development of new industries and expansion of those already existing.

Society in the Strathtay area, like most of Highland Scotland, would generally have consisted of people who were born, raised and died never having travelled more than ten miles in their lifetime. This now changed; the county town of Perth was only an hour away, hitherto difficult visits to Dundee, Edinburgh or Glasgow could now be undertaken as a day trip. Equally too, due to the resurgence of interest in the Scottish Highlands thanks mainly to Queen Victoria's love of Balmoral, people were being attracted to the area, resulting in the development of housing at Taybridge Terrace and Taybridge Drive; due to the railway, residing in Aberfeldy was now an option and Highland living was no longer remote and out of touch. It was also the means whereby local people and families could leave the area to seek a livelihood in other Scottish cities, down south or as a conduit to the seaport to sail to the many far flung parts of the empire for a new life. Lastly the railway was the means of conveying men to war, whether South Africa or the two World Wars of 1914 – 1918 and 1939 – 1945, many sadly never to return as the roll call of remembrance on the many war memorials in the area can readily testify.

Due entirely to railway development a new burgeoning industry was developing – tourism. As the introductory article from the *Perthshire Advertiser* stated:

"take a trip to Aberfeldy; for the beauties of Strathtay, like many other beauties in this world of ours must be seen to be fully appreciated".

From the very outset they did take trips as these two articles from the *Perthshire Advertiser* firstly of July 22nd 1891 writes:

Visitors:- On Saturday a considerable number of visitors arrived from Glasgow determined to spend "Fair Week" among the hills. As Dundee holidays approach the demand for lodgings increases, and the landladies are at their wits end to find accommodation for the number of applicants. Three special trains are to arrive on Saturday from Dundee and for the sake of the many excursions and the hay, the great part of which is now cut, it is hoped the weather will be fine.

The article of July 29th 1891 is as follows:-

Visitors: Our little town is this week thronged with strangers mostly from Dundee. The behaviour of the excursionists is admirable.

The paper also published for information the Highland Railway timetable of trains to Aberfeldy showing whether north or south connections were available at Ballinluig.

The Highland Railway Company in conjunction with the North British Railway and the Caledonian Railway for several years organised tours described as being by rock, wood and glen and by river, loch and sea; their 1880 programme of arrangements lists the two examples shown opposite. With the advent of the Loch Tay steamers, coaches ran between Aberfeldy and Kenmore to connect with the steamers.

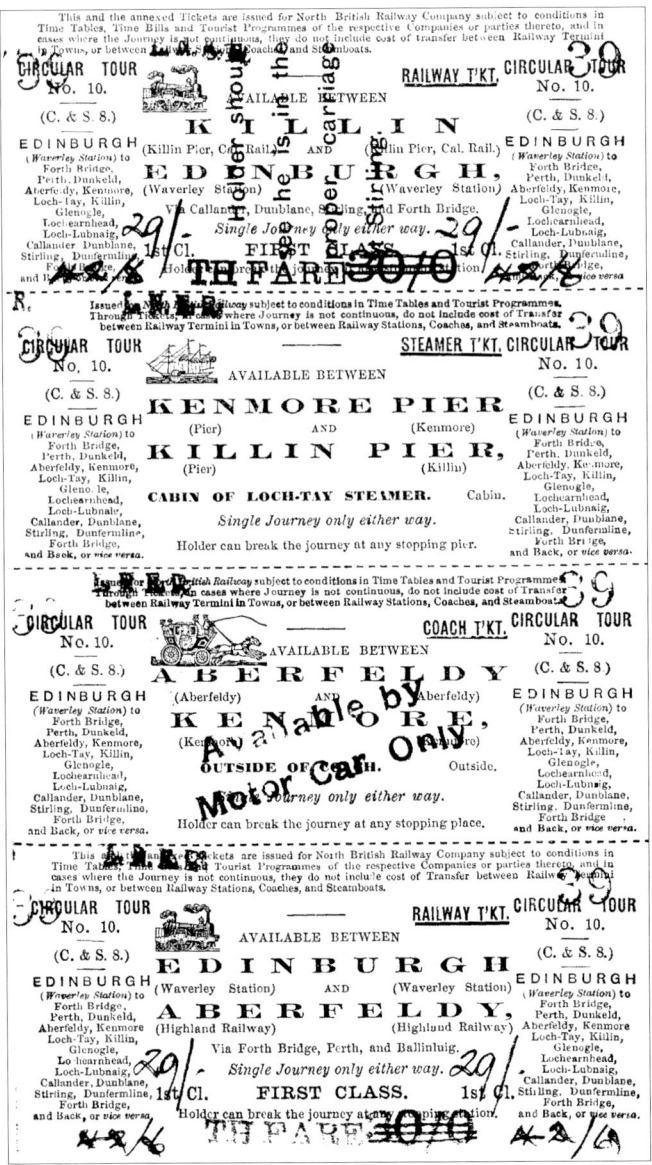

Part of a circular tour ticket with separate portions for each part of the journey. These were folded concertina fashion.

A Highland Railway handbook for the early 1900s describes Aberfeldy as a village of considerable size, having excellent hotel accommodation at the Breadalbane Arms, the Station Hotel and the Palace Hotel with, additionally, ample residential accommodation for those who prefer it. It also promotes the area by extolling the virtues of the Birks of Aberfeldy, the local nine hole golf course, tennis courts and bowling green. Lastly it suggests that tourists should avail themselves of the new motor coach service to Fortingall and Glen Lyon and in particular of the motor coach to Kenmore thence by the steamer up Loch Tay to Killin with the enticing possibility of further travel to Oban and the Western Highlands. The railway company did, therefore, create and further encourage this new phenomenon.

A delightful book *Never an Old Tin Hut* published to celebrate the centenary of the golf club at Aberfeldy describes its early fortunes as being highly dependant on the railway bringing visitors to the area alongside the cheap fare deals to golfers travelling more than five miles. The golf course is still thriving in the 21st century, now an eighteen hole course thanks to the building of an innovative and iconic bridge across the Tay to access the added nine holes. Tourism still exists. The Birks, still beautiful and well maintained, Loch Tay, golf at Taymouth Castle and salmon fishing all thrive, thanks initially to that new communication system born in 1865.

Commerce, likewise, also developed with the advent of railway communication enabling produce, livestock and goods to be transported both in and out of the area. James Fisher's book *Memories of an Aberfeldy Childhood* tells of a particularly busy goods department, dealing with in particular a thriving timber trade, farm produce especially seed potatoes, most shop supplies and the import of coal to three coal merchants who served the area; the national chain of John Menzies later opened a kiosk which acted as both retail and wholesale suppliers of newspapers and magazines. Merchandise and commodities previously unobtainable or not readily available were now in the local shops thanks to the railway's arrival. Existing firms expanded and totally new enterprises were created.

The field beside the buffer stops was a popular place for photographing the station. This view appears to have been taken in Highland Railway days. The four and six wheel coaches are all Highland designs, seeing out their last years on branch line work. (HRS collection)

First amongst them was the construction of Aberfeldy distillery, completed in 1898. Whilst whisky production did exist in the area it was on a small scale and often illicit, but due to a worldwide increase in popularity major expansion and rationalisation was taking place. Aberfeldy distillery, built by Dewar's, was blessed on two counts, a railway line adjacent enabling the provision of dedicated sidings and the waters of the Pitilie burn which were a vital element in the arcane alchemy that is Scotch whisky distilling. The railway enabled the barrels of malt whisky to be transported directly to Perth for storage and blending at the massive Dewar's complex at Glasgow Road/Glover Street, which incidentally was located opposite the old Highland locomotive shed to the north side of the Glasgow Road railway bridge. The distillery is still in production with an annual output of around two million litres; it is also home to "Dewar's World of Whisky" a high quality tourist attraction. The whisky itself receives high praise in Michael Jackson's whisky companion, the 15 year old Aberfeldy single malt is especially worth tasting and described as firm, oily, cleanly fruity, vigorous, best served in its teens, after dinner or with a book at bedtime.

Another new development was the unique aerial ropeway which brought down stone for railway ballast and road metalling. This was quarried and crushed into different grades at Gatehouse Quarry, two miles south and one thousand feet up Grandtully Hill. The ropeway was supported on metal pylons, 30 to 40 feet high spaced 100 yards apart. A continuous steel rope ran over pulleys carrying metal buckets each of 3cwt capacity. The stone was delivered directly to railway wagons or the County Council road metal bank which was situated between the water tank and engine shed to the east of Aberfeldy station; from there it was dispatched in the Council's own transport to various locations throughout north Perthshire for road making and road repair. The quarry and ropeway was estimated to have operated for thirty to forty years from its inception in 1904.

Changes also took place to farming practices as a consequence of railways as the days of drove roads and trysts were now over. The carriage of livestock by train created local markets adjacent to railheads. To this end in 1883 at the behest of Lord Breadalbane a new and larger market was built, sited at Hope Street and Market Street. It is my understanding that this was run in its entirety by the world famous auctioneers McDonald Fraser, earning renown as the creators of the famous annual Perth bull sales. This market was usually held monthly with special sales of cattle in the spring and a large sheep sale in December, generally noted for being held in snowy weather. The spring sale was renowned for quality beef cattle brought from as far as Killin and Glen Lyon for auction, thence for shipment by rail to other parts of Perthshire, Angus and Aberdeenshire.

P & J Haggart tweed manufacturers were established initially in 1807 at Acharn on south Loch Tay side; as a consequence of the railway's arrival, they relocated to Aberfeldy in 1882, building a small factory at Keltnyburn and opening a shop in Dunkeld Street. The firm were manufacturers of high quality tweeds, much of which was exported to places such as Germany and the United States. The Highland Railway guidebook describes the firm thus:-

> *In the neighbourhood are the famous Breadalbane mills – The property of Messrs P & J Haggart – where native wool is wrought into blankets, plaiding, winceys, clan tartans, tweed and crumb cloths. These mills are well worthy of a visit. Messrs Haggart hold royal warrants as woollen manufacturers to their majesties the King and Queen, and other members of the royal family, and this is a guarantee of the excellence of the various articles produced in their mills. Since the opening of the line, a considerable impetus has been given to the local trade in this and other directions.*

Impetus given in other directions leads to the final part of this section. Consider initially newspaper reports on the list of visitors published at the turn of the 19th-20th century, where you will find some eighty establishments listed containing up to 250 names which excluded family and servants, so a figure of nearer 300 is probably more accurate. Reflect also on the painting "Perth station, coming South", by George Earl, now displayed in the National Railway Museum at York, which vividly depicts the type of visitor who came to the area, the painting showing the assembled mass of passengers, mainly families, their servants and dogs, associated gun bags, fishing tackle and trophies awaiting the express to return south, having just travelled down from the Highlands. The list of visitors in many cases was akin to Who's Who or Debretts. This huge influx of people and others previously referred to created a new requirement, the necessity for laundering. A local Aberfeldy grocer James Fisher spotted this need, had the vision and energy and founded Fisher's Laundry. Whilst it never used the railway directly, it served the local houses and hotels initially employing horse drawn conveyances and its formation was directly due to the major influx of visitors to the area brought about by the railway. During the Second World War they obtained a laundering contract for the military and naval forces stationed in Oban and the Sound of Mull, where flying boat and naval bases were involved in convoy protection. Laundered items were taken by road to either Killin or Killin Junction for further despatch by rail to Oban using the Callander and Oban line. Fishers are still a thriving business based in Aberfeldy, with branches in Cupar, Perth and Newcastle specialising in hotel and restaurant linen and workwear laundering/rental. Thus from initially serving a local need, large oaks and small acorns seems an apt description.

Many other firms, shops, hotels, boarding houses and the like grew out of the branch line's arrival in Aberfeldy, Grandtully and Strathtay and were sustained by its existence; it did indeed bring about considerable change, both social and economic.

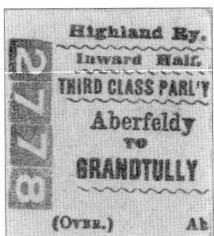

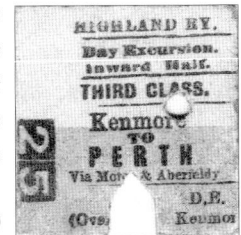

The Highland, like all railways, had to operate at least one train a day at a fare of not more than 1d per mile. These were referred to as Parliamentary Trains - abbreviated in the ticket on the left to 'Parl'y'. Quite often all trains carried Third Class passengers at this rate. The ticket on the right was issued in conjunction with the road motor service to Kenmore.

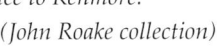

(John Roake collection)

Operating the Line

The Aberfeldy branch was run by only three companies over its near 100 year existence. On opening the Highland Railway company was the owner of the line; the amalgamation of the Inverness & Perth with the Inverness & Aberdeen Junction railways having been passed by Parliament only four days previously on 29th June 1865; its constructor narrowly missed out running the branch as a consequence. On 1st January 1923 the Highland became part of the London, Midland & Scottish Railway (LMS) the biggest of the new big four railway operating companies created after World War I under the Railways Act of 1921. Lastly the branch became part of the Scottish region of British Railways on January 1st 1948 as a result of the post war nationalisation of the railway industry, continuing under its control until ultimate closure in 1965.

Throughout its operation very little significant change took place to the structure apart from, firstly, the opening in 1935 by the LMS of Balnaguard halt 2¼ miles from Ballinluig. It comprised a very basic wooden shelter, a sleepered platform to one side only, nameplate and oil lamps. To this day, however, the now badly worn enamelled sign stating "Balnaguard – LMS halt platform" is still attached to a building in the hamlet showing the route to the halt, a grass path between buildings and fields taking you to the overbridge which lay to the west. The track bed towards Ballinluig is still clearly visible and the site is now a silage store for a local farmer. Secondly was the formation of two new sidings at Aberfeldy distillery, strangely like the Balnaguard sign still partly remaining as a site for the static display of a tank engine as part of the Dewar's visitor experience.

Locomotive power on the line was through almost its entire existence provided by tank engines because there were no turntables at either end. In 1871, no.12 *Belladrum*, a 2-2-2 was rebuilt as a tank engine for use on the line. It was not very successful there and was replaced in 1880 by a new Jones 2-4-0 tank, no.17, which was then named *Breadalbane*, changed to *Aberfeldy* in 1886. It was given larger tanks for this duty. Later, no.103, a 4-4-0T of the Yankee Tank class, was sent to work the branch and

Aberfeldy signal box in 1962. This was a standard Highland Railway design but with a low floor instead of the normal level several feet above the ground.

(Keith Fenwick)

The branch train has arrived at Aberfeldy sometime in the 1950s and passengers and parcels are being unloaded. The locomotive will be uncoupled from the front of the train and then run round to detach the goods wagons and shunt them into the sidings ready for unloading.

this too received larger tanks. A few engines were also utilised in Highland days, including the 0-6-4 Banking Tanks used on the hill from Blair Atholl. During most of the LMS regime and up to 1961 the commonest locomotive power was the McIntosh Caledonian "439" class 0-4-4 tanks. Diesel traction should have taken over in 1961, but locomotive availability delayed this and BR Class 4 2-6-4Ts were used for a short time before B.R./Sulzer type 2 diesels took.

Management of locomotives and the Aberfeldy shed was from the Highland Railway southern terminus at Perth, originally from the HR shed situated adjacent to the Glasgow Road just north of Perth General Station. This shed became Perth North in LMS days, closing eventually in 1938 after the new Perth South shed was completed. Perth South, 29A in L.M.S. days and 63A in B.R. days, then became responsible for the Aberfeldy sub-shed.

After the very early years when only three or four trains travelled the

Black 5 No.44796 at Aberfeldy with, on the footplate, driver Willie Lees and fireman Charlie Cairney. Guards Willie Matheson and Dave Stewart stand at the rear of the group and the man in the middle front could be Willie Anderson, the clerk, but the identity of the other two is not known.

(Mrs L Fischbacher collection)

BALLINLUIG AND ABERFELDY—Week Days only — Table 412

													SX		SO						SO	
Glasgow (Buch. Street)...dep.	...	...	7 20		10 5	...	...		1 40	...		3 5		...		6 8		9 0	...
Edinburgh (Princes St.)... ,,	.	.	7 0		9 25	.	.		b1 23	.		.	.	...		w5 25		3 45	...
Dundee (West)............... ,,	.	.	8 15		10 45	.	.		2 55	.		4 45	.	.		7 5		9 40	...
Perth........................... ,,	5 45	.	9 25		11 45	.	.		3 40	.	4 0	5 35	.	.		8 5		10 43	...
Inverness .... ,,	G11 20	.	.		S08 35	.	11 5	.	.	.	.	.	.	.	.	.	.	.	.
Ballinluig........ ....dep.	7 40	.	10 20		12 35	.	2 35	...	4 28	.	5 40	6 30	.	...		9 0	.	11 35	...
Balnaguard........................ ,,	7 43	.	10 23		12 38	.	2 38	...	B4 31	.	5 43	6 33	.	.		E	.	E	
Grandtully........................ ,,	7 53	.	10 31		12 45	...	2 46	.	4 38	.	5 50	6 40	.	...		E	.	E	
Aberfeldy.................... arr.	8 6	.	10 52		12 54	.	2 57	.	4 47	.	5 59	6 49	.	...		9 18	.	11 53	
	MO			MX															SO	
Aberfeldy ....dep.	6 57	.	7 4	.	.	8 52	...	12 2	...	1 30	...	...	3 57	5 10	.	...	11 0	...
Grandtully............................ ,,	7 7	.	7 12	.	.	9 0	...	12 11	.	1 38	.	.	4 0	5 18	.	...	11 8	
Balnaguard........................ ,,	7 17	.	7 18	.	.	9 6	.	12 18	.	1 44	.	.	4 11	5 24	.	.	11 14	
Ballinluig.................... arr.	7 23	.	7 23	.	...	9 11	.	12 24	.	1 49	...	...	4 16	5 29	.	...	11 19	...
Inverness ....arr.	.	.	.	.	...	.	.	3 46	...	.	...	7 41	.	.	.	...	.	...
Perth........................... ,,	8 19	.	8 19	.	.	10 9	.	S01 21	...	2 45	.	.	.	6 29	.	.	.	...
Dundee (West).............. ,,	9 26	.	9 26	.	.	11 18	.	S02 10	.	3 55	.	.	.	7 7	.	.	.	...
Edinburgh (Princes St.)... ,,	10 55	.	10 55	.	.	d2 24	.	S04 38	.	.	.	.	.	c9 42	.	.	.	
Glasgow (Buch. Street)... arr.	10 15	.	10 15	.	.	d2 7	.	S04 24	.	f5 9	.	.	.	e9 14	.	.	.	

B—Calls on notice to take up or set down.
E—Calls on notice to set down.
G—Saturday nights and Sunday nights excepted.
MO—Mondays only.   MX—Mondays excepted.
SO—Saturdays only. SX—Saturdays excepted.
b—1.10 p.m. on Saturdays.
c—9.49 p.m. daily until October 2nd, inclusive, and on Saturdays thereafter.
d—Arrives Edinburgh (Princes Street) at 1.45 p.m. and Glasgow (Buchanan Street) at 12.42 p.m. on Saturdays.
e—9.2 p.m. until October 2nd, inclusive.
f—4.47 p.m. until October 2nd, inclusive.
w—Waverley Station, via Larbert.

LMS timetable which was to have applied from 25th September 1939 until the following summer. This timetable was published before war was declared and was replaced by an emergency one.

BR Scottish Region Timetable for the summer of 1954. Some of the footnotes refer to the Dornoch line timetable which was on the same page.

Ballinluig and Aberfeldy — Table 122
WEEKDAYS ONLY

Mls		a.m.		a.m.		a.m.				Sats only a.m.		p.m		p.m				p.m	
..	115 Glasgow (Buchanan St.)lev.	..	..	7 15	..	1015 Z	..	..	..	..	..	1 45	..	..	..	..	..	6 10	..
..	115 Edinburgh (Waverley)	..	..	7 40	..	1012	..	..	..	..	..	2 5	..	..	..	..	..	SP22	..
..	115 Inverness	..	..	..	..	..	..	..	..	11 0	..	11 0L	..	..	..	..	..	3 40	..
..	115 Perth	5 50	..	9 25	..	1215	..	..	..	..	..	3 50	..	4 10	..	..	..	8 10	..
..	Ballinluig .... lev.	7 40	..	1028	..	1 5	..	..	..	2 35	..	4 38	..	5 50	..	..	..	9 10	..
1¼	Balnaguard	7 45	..	1033	..	1 10	..	..	..	2 39	..	4 42	..	5 54	..	..	..	9d14	..
4¼	Grandtully	7 52	..	1040	..	1 17	..	..	..	..	..	4 48	..	6 0	..	..	..	9d20	..
8¼	Aberfeldy .... arr.	8 9	..	1053	..	1 30	..	..	..	2 52	..	4 57	..	6 9	..	..	..	9 29	..

Aberfeldy and Ballinluig
WEEKDAYS ONLY

		a.m.		a.m.		p.m				Sats only p.m		p.m				p.m		p.m	
Aberfeldy .... lev.	6 41	..	8 45	..	1210	..	..	..	1 55	..	4 7	..	..	..	5 15	..	8 0	..
Grandtully	6 49	..	8 56	..	1230	..	..	..	2 3	..	..	..	..	..	5 23	..	8d11	..
Balnaguard	6 55	..	9 5	..	1237	..	..	..	2 9	..	4 19	..	..	..	5 29	..	..	..
Ballinluig .... arr.	7 1	..	9 11	..	1243	..	..	..	2 15	..	4 25	..	..	..	5 35	..	8 24	..
115 Perth .... arr.	8 0	..	10 9	..	2 46	..	..	..	3 5	..	..	..	..	..	6 34	..	..	..
115 Inverness	..	..	3E25	..	5 37	..	..	..	..	..	7 55	..	..	..	..	..	..	..
115 Edinburgh (Waverley)	9 52	..	1 50	..	5H1	..	..	..	5 1	..	..	..	..	..	8 39	..	..	..
115 Glasgow (Buch. St.) arr.	10 5	..	1222	..	4*31X	..	..	..	4 57	..	..	..	..	..	9F12	..	..	..

* Saturdays only † Except Saturdays
A Trains stop at Cambusavie on notice at Mound or Skelbo or when Passengers on platform to be taken up
d Stops to take up or set down on notice at previous stopping Station
E Saturdays 2-56 p.m
F Saturdays 8-52 a.m
H Saturdays from 26th June arrives 4-48 p.m
L Leave 11-20 a.m from 26th June
P Princes Street Station
X Begins 26th June
Z Saturdays 10-30 a.m

line in each direction, the branch was soon served by six trains daily in each direction, variations mainly taking place in winter, on Saturdays and with the addition of summer specials. By the early years of the 20th century there were ten trains each way. The line, too, was like other small branches in that up to half the trains ran as mixed, comprising both passenger and goods rolling stock, this practice continuing right up to closure. Journey times were 20 to 25 minutes. The passenger trains were timed to connect with the Perth – Blair Atholl local services and many of the through trains to and from Inverness allowing connection northwards and southwards. The final timetable in 1964/65 showed five trains from Aberfeldy, starting at 6.35am with the last one at 5.25pm, plus an extra in the afternoon on Saturdays. There were six in the opposite direction, the last one giving a connection from the 6.8pm from Perth. Passengers connecting at Ballinluig usually had to wait for about 5 minutes. Journeys to Perth took between 1 hour 15 minutes and 1 hour 30 minutes. By then, no attempt seems to have been made to provide connections northwards.

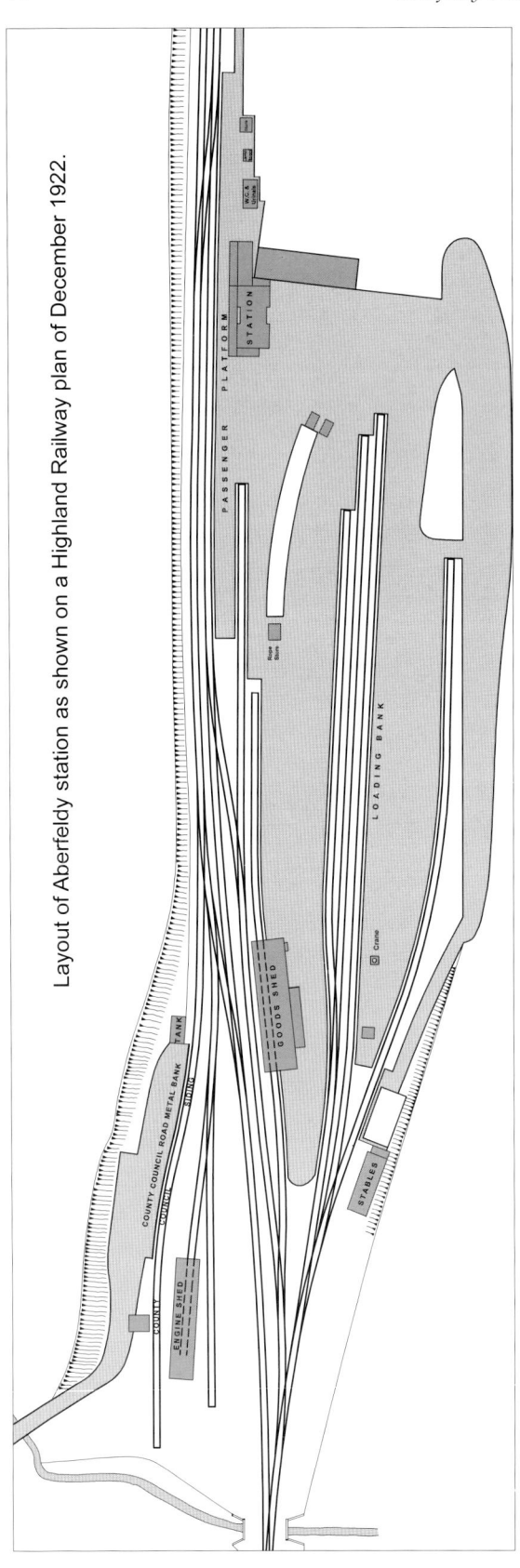

Layout of Aberfeldy station as shown on a Highland Railway plan of December 1922.

Goods traffic from Aberfeldy was carried by mixed trains and was either dropped off at Grandtully, one train daily generally performing this function, or more usually left at Ballinluig awaiting connection southwards or northwards. Goods to Aberfeldy were generally part of local mixed goods trains operating out of Perth.

The make up of trains in Highland days is illustrated by this extract from the carriage formations for 1st July 1903 : 2 Firsts, 2 Thirds and Brake Van on all Trains. Composite Carriage to and from Perth by 9.40am, also 1.42 and 4.50pm Trains ex Aberfeldy, and by 10.34am; also by 1.13 and 5.40pm Trains ex Ballinluig. These would all be 4 or 6-wheelers but later bogie coaches were cascaded from more important services. By the 1950s, one or two coaches sufficed for the traffic on offer.

Through coaches were run to and from Perth for many years as illustrated for 1903. These had disappeared by the early 1950s, maybe as a wartime economy measure, but reappeared in the mid-1950s and continued on one train each way until closure.

Notwithstanding the apparently straightforward and consistent operating timetables the branch was not surprisingly subject to both general and specific regulation. Some examples are shown in the extracts from the 1920 Appendix to the Highland Railway Working Timetable on page 41.

The branch was single track having no passing places or loops, consequently only one train was allowed between Ballinluig and Aberfeldy. For the majority of its existence one train running back and forth was sufficient to handle all the traffic.

The Highland Railway operated its lines to strict timetables with the aid of the electric telegraph to ensure that only one train was on each single line at any time. Out of course running or special trains had to be sanctioned by telegraph from Inverness. Despite the potential for mistakes inherent

Extracts from Highland Railway Appendix to Working Timetable 1920

1. No two engines in steam, unless coupled together, are to be between any adjoining respective tablet or telegraph block stations, at any one and the same time, viz:- Ballinluig and Aberfeldy.

2. ABERFELDY DISTILLERY SIDING : This siding situated about half a mile south of Aberfeldy station, is controlled by a ground frame locked by tablet, and will be worked by Aberfeldy branch train engine and men under electric tablet regulations. Stationmaster, Aberfeldy to send a weekly report on the working of this siding.

3. HORSES AND CARRIAGES : Can be loaded and unloaded at Aberfeldy, Grandtully, Ballinluig.

4. WAGONS LEFT BEHIND ON ABERFELDY BRANCH : When, from any cause, the ordinary trains do not clear out Aberfeldy, Grandtully or Ballinluig, the stationmasters at Aberfeldy and Ballinluig will arrange for a special train being run at a suitable time, under tablet regulations, to work forward the traffic. Unless the demands are urgent, a special train should not be run with less than eight wagons. In every case advice of the extra trains must be sent to the traffic manager.

5. CARTERS UNLOADING WAGONS IN STATION YARDS AND SIDINGS

Accidents resulting in serious personal injury to carters and others, at work in station yards, have occurred, from want of care on the part of those engaged in shunting operations.

It will be the duty of shunters, guards and other servants of the company directing shunting operations to warn such persons by word of mouth before signalling the engine driver to move any wagon near which they may be engaged.

Considerable difficulty had been experienced in getting carters and others to desist from unloading wagons which are about to be shunted or moved within the station yards or sidings and as, notwithstanding the orders which have been issued from time to time on the subject, fatal accidents have occurred to carters while so engaged, the special attention of stationmasters, shunters, guards, and others is drawn to this important matter, and they are requested, with the view of ensuring the safety of the carters, and of supporting the shunters, and others engaged in shunting operations, that, in the event of any carter refusing or delaying, when asked, to quit a wagon which requires to be moved, the request should be repeated in presence of two witnesses, and that, if not at once complied with, the name and address of the carter so refusing or delaying shall be taken, with the view to his prosecution under the company's Bye-laws.

Carts being loaded from wagons must not be allowed to be backed close on to the vehicles, but so placed that, in the event of any movement no damage would occur. When shunting operations are to commence, party in charge must see that carts, etc, are quite clear, and due warning given before permission to shunt is authorised.

Stationmasters and others in authority will take measures to satisfy themselves from time to time that the above instructions are being attended to, reporting all cases of violation thereof.

6. ENGINE WATERING STATIONS ETC : Ballinluig goods yard and Aberfeldy Loco shed.

7. PERMANENT WAY INSPECTORS : Peter Turnbull, covering Blair Atholl to Stanley, and Aberfeldy branch and living at Dunkeld.

8. TELEGRAPH LINEMEN : James Ross, covering Dalwhinnie to Perth and Aberfeldy branch, residing Blair Atholl.

9. SIGNAL FITTERS, A. Cooke, Murthly to Dalnaspidal and Aberfeldy Branch, residing Blair Atholl.

10. LOCOMOTIVE DISTRICTS ETC, under Mr J.M. Nisbet at Perth. From Pitlochry (exclusive of station) to Perth and Aberfeldy branch. Engine sheds at Perth and Aberfeldy. Carriage and wagon inspection on Aberfeldy branch to be done by drivers and locomotive staff.

in this system, the Highland railwaymen were very conscientious and careful and no accidents were ever recorded. On the Aberfeldy branch problems could occur if the main line trains were running late, a relatively common event.

At Aberfeldy, the points would be worked by hand. The first edition OS map shows two signals, one at the approach to the station for arriving trains, the other at the platform end to signal departures.

Despite the Highland thinking this was a safe and economical way of operating the branch, it was obliged after 1889 to introduce block signalling and to interlock points and signals. As considerable capital expenditure was required to make this change, the work was spread over several years. In 1892, a signal box was installed on the south side of the line to control all the points except the crossover near the buffer stop which allowed engines to run round the coaches after arrival. New signals were also installed. Tyer's No.6 Electric Train Tablet instruments were installed at Aberfeldy and Ballinluig and the driver now had to be in possession of the tablet as authority to use the single line. Similarly, a small signal box was installed at the distillery controlling the points at that location, this too being released by the tablet.

The use of the tablet now meant that it was possible to run two trains in succession in the same direction on the branch. As evidenced from timetables normal running would not require this facility, it would only be needed on the operation of specials.

By the 1930s, economies were required and changes were made to the signalling. To save the cost of a "dedicated" qualified signalman at Aberfeldy, "one engine in steam" working was introduced,

Railwaymen and local workers are represented in this group on the platform at Aberfeldy in the late Edwardian era. From the left, two porters, Ronald McDonald from the Breadalbane Hotel and Peter McDougall from the Station Hotel, postman Danny McDougall with his mailcart who in those days made three deliveries daily starting before 8am. Third right is bellringer Ben Kerr and second right is baker John Kerr, who later joined the Royal Canadian Mounted Police and attained the rank of sergeant. The locomotive is an 0-4-4T Yankee Tank; no.102 is known to have worked the branch between 1906 and 1910. (G Gregory collection)

Driver Willie Lees, guard Dave Stewart and fireman Charlie Cairney stand in front of Black 5 No.44796 at Ballinluig in the 1950s. (Mrs L Fischbacher collection)

using a train staff. The tablet equipment was retained, nonetheless, if occasional heavy traffic demanded. Unless the train was in the station, points and signals were set to allow the train to leave and arrive at the platform. When the train was in the station, the train staff released the lever frame, thus allowing points and signals to operate. The distillery box was replaced with an open ground frame, now controlled either by the staff or the tablet. These arrangements continued until closure.

Another railway enterprise was located in Aberfeldy, namely the camping coach. Best described as the forerunner of static caravans these converted carriages provided reasonably priced self catering family holiday accommodation. It would appear from articles that the LMS were present in Aberfeldy pre-war, the coach returning in 1952 as a B.R. Scottish region camping coach. The Aberfeldy coach DMSC3 was a converted L.N.W.R. third corridor carriage, its conversion work having been undertaken at St. Rollox, Glasgow; this coach saw service from 1952 until withdrawn at end of the 1963 holiday season.

Aberfeldy distillery still has a connection with the railway in the exhibits beside the building. These consist of a wagon with whisky barrels and a tank locomotive which came from Dailuaine Distillery near Aberlour on Speyside. Whisky barrels were usually carried upright in high-sides wagons, not as loaded here. (C J Stewart)

ABERFELDY STATION BUILDING

ELEVATION TO PLATFORM

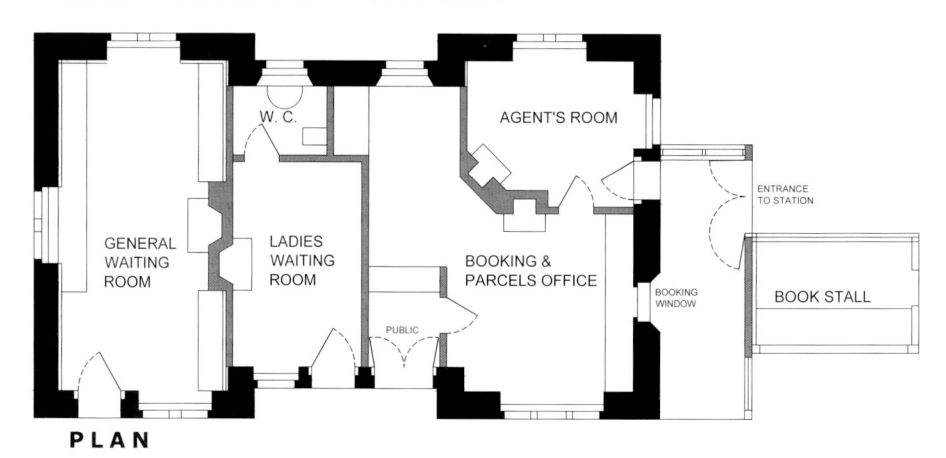

- GENERAL WAITING ROOM
- W. C.
- LADIES WAITING ROOM
- PUBLIC
- AGENT'S ROOM
- BOOKING & PARCELS OFFICE
- BOOKING WINDOW
- ENTRANCE TO STATION
- BOOK STALL

PLAN

The attractive proportions of the building at Aberfeldy are still evident in this view from the 1960s, not long before closure. The bookstall is at the far end of the building. (Norris Forrest/GNSRA)

Fatalities, Fires, Flood and Findings

In this present age accidents and fatalities are the exception rather than the norm; this was not the case in the early days of railways. In the latter part of the nineteenth century it was not uncommon for around 1000 fatalities and 6000 injuries to be recorded per annum, the majority of deaths being to employees with trespassers, including, sadly, suicides to a lesser extent. The Highland Railway and in particular the Aberfeldy branch had, statistically, a lower than average incidence of these but did nonetheless experience some such tragic events, as the following newspaper articles show.

In 1879 the *Perthshire Advertiser* of April 10th reported the following incident:-

On Monday morning while Mr John Saunders, Grocer, was superintending the unloading of a quantity of seeds at the Aberfeldy railway station, he was caught between the buffers of two wagons, sustaining serious abdominal injury. Good hopes are entertained on his recovery.

However on April 18th the following was, sadly, recorded:

Fatal accident:- Mr John Saunders, Grocer; who was recently crushed between the buffers of two wagons at Aberfeldy Railway station died on Thursday morning in consequence of the severe internal injuries he had sustained. Mr Saunders, who was a widower, leaves a young family.

The *Perthshire Courier* of 17th February 1885 published the following report:-

Fatal railway accident:- A farmer named James McFarlane residing at Sketewan about two miles below Grandtully station was found dead on the Aberfeldy branch line about eight o'clock of Friday night. It appears that the deceased was seen standing on the retaining wall parapet immediately below his farm steading as the 5.55pm train from Ballinluig was approaching Grandtully, and it is conjectured that he may have become giddy and fallen over as the train was passing.

On 19th October 1886 the *Perthshire Courier* contained the following feature:-

Man killed on Highland Railway:- James Garvie, surfaceman on the Aberfeldy branch of the Highland Railway was killed on Wednesday night on the main line about 200 yards north of Ballinluig distant signal. It is supposed that Garvie was run over by the 3pm express mail from Inverness due at Ballinluig at 6.30. The body was badly mangled. Deceased was unmarried and about 50 years of age.

Lastly a less serious incident was reported in the *Perthshire Advertiser* of July 14th 1881:-

On Saturday last the engine on the Aberfeldy branch line, while engaged in shunting some wagons, went off the rails causing a complete block, and delaying both mails and passengers for upwards of three hours.

Fire made its presence felt on several occasions during the lines existence, the station building at Aberfeldy being twice destroyed by its ravages, and the Aberfeldy engine shed, too, being once burnt to the ground.

The original wooden structure that served as the station building was totally devastated on December 4th 1878. Its reconstruction generated considerable interest as the *Perthshire Courier* of 28th January 1879 recorded:-

New Station:- The plans and specifications for the erection of the new railway station are now ready and building operations will probably be commenced as soon as favourable weather sets in. The buildings are to be of stone, and it is expected they will be finished by the beginning of July.

Continuing on 18th February 1879 the *Courier* reported that:-

New Railway station:- The contract for the mason work of the new station has been secured by Messrs McDonald and Blaikie, Builders. Building operations will be commenced shortly.

Lastly in this episode the *Courier* of 14th October reported:-

New station:- The new station at Aberfeldy is now approaching completion. It will be remembered that on 14th December 1878 the wooden erection which formerly did service as station house was utterly destroyed by fire. In the beginning of April the new building was begun, and notwithstanding the severe spring progressed rapidly, the whole work being all but finished in the course of six months. It is a neat building of gothic architecture and contains every accommodation. The dimensions are 45, 25 and 9 feet – length, breadth and height respectively. The cost is estimated at £750. The architects employed were Messrs Paterson and Craig, Inverness; Messrs Blaikie & McDonald executed the mason work (the ornamental finishing being done in a most masterly and workmanlike manner); Mr Stewart, Cruden, the Joiner; and Mr James McBeath, Pitlochry, the plaster work.

Fifty years later history repeated itself the station building was again destroyed by fire as the *Perthshire Advertiser* of June 12th 1929 recorded:

New Station Premises:- After what seems to be considerable delay, workmen are now busily engaged reconstructing the railway station premises which were burnt to the ground on the morning of 8th January last. The work of rebuilding the station is to be hurried forward as quickly as possible and every effort will be made to have the work practically completed by the end of July. The old walls are not entirely being pulled down, but the new station is to be of modern type, in keeping with the importance of Aberfeldy as a terminal station and adapted to meet the requirements of present day passengers and general traffic. In many respects the building will have many conveniences for the travelling public and staff not possessed by the old station. The contractors are the well-known firm of Messrs W. Taylor and Sons Ltd, Glasgow.

The original timber built single-road engine shed was also destroyed by fire in 1902; it was an insubstantial wooden affair, which surprisingly was rebuilt in timber. It did, however, survive until closure of the branch in 1965.

Whilst experiencing fatalities and the ravages of fire the most widely reported incident experienced during the history of the line was the Balnaguard derailment caused by flooding. The event took place on Friday 20th November 1959, when the 6.41am up passenger train from Aberfeldy to Ballinluig derailed approximately three-quarters of a mile west of Balnaguard where 25 feet of embankment, 16 feet deep had been washed away. A period of intense rainfall had preceded the incident, 3.02 inches of rain, 75% of the monthly average, falling in the 24 hours up to 9.00 am on the day of the incident. These factors alone contributing to the washout. Of significance, nonetheless, are some of the conclusions and remarks by Colonel J.R.H. Robertson, author of the original report into the accident in which he states that he was satisfied that the length of line was properly inspected and well maintained, that arrangements for cleaning out the ditches were sensible and conscientiously carried out. He further stated that in his view events of 19th/20th November 1959 could not reasonably have been foreseen or better guarded against and moreover wrote that the train crew were properly alert and could not have prevented the accident or lessened the damage. He concluded by saying they behaved commendably after the incident and that no one was in any way to blame for this derailment. Testament to the permanent way crew and enginemen indeed made even more impressive in that the

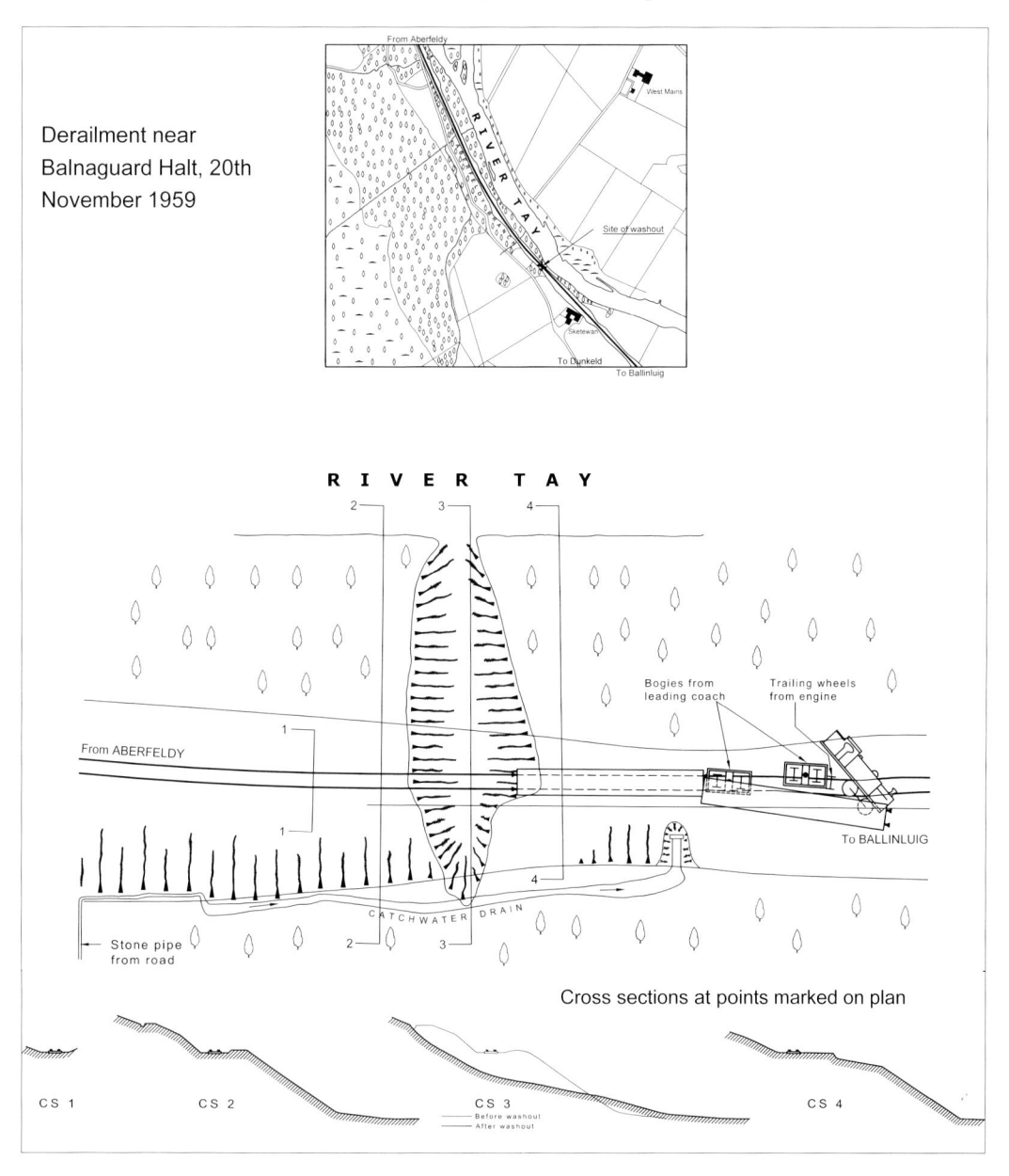

Derailment near Balnaguard Halt, 20th November 1959

Cross sections at points marked on plan

line re-opened on 30th November 1959, ten days after the derailment and washout; further evidence of the pride and professionalism of railwaymen.

An interesting court case concerning the Aberfeldy branch is found in an 1897 book entitled *The Law of Railways Applicable to Scotland*, where in chapter VIII "Questions as to fares and tickets and the right to remove from carriages" the following can be found:-

> *A distinction must then be taken between the right to apprehend and detain under Section 97 of the [Railways Clauses Consolidation (Scotland)] Act of 1845, and the right to remove under Section 102. To entitle him to start with a train a passenger must not only have a ticket which he maintains to be sufficient, but one that is in fact the right one for the contemplated, or possible, journey. These propositions by the case of Menzies, (Highland Railway Co. v Sir Robert Menzies (1878)) in which the circumstances were these: The regulations of the company set forth that a special class of return tickets would be issued on Sunday, "available on day of issue only", that "local return tickets other*

than the above are not recognised on Sundays", and that on Fridays return tickets would be issued "between all stations on the main line and branches, ... by the last train of the day available to return on the following Saturday or Monday". The by-laws and regulations also bore that "no passenger will be allowed to enter any carriages used on the railway, or to travel therein upon the railway, unless furnished by the company with a ticket specifying the class of carriage and the stations for conveyance between which such tickets issued . . . . Any passenger travelling without a ticket as aforesaid, shall be required to pay the fare from the station whence the train originally started to the end of the journey. Any passenger using or attempting to use a ticket on any day for which such ticket is not available . . . . is hereby subjected to a penalty not exceeding 40s." These by-laws and regulations were printed and published in the time-tables and posted on the walls of the company's stations, including Aberfeldy. The pursuer purchased a return ticket at Aberfeldy for the last train on Friday, for which he paid the reduced fare. It bore on its face the words "Saturday Fare", and the names of the stations. On Sunday morning he took his seat at Perth in the only train that day that stopped at Ballinluig, the junction for the Aberfeldy line, upon which no trains ran on a Sunday, intending to get out at Ballinluig and walk on. The ticket collector challenged him, and said he could not travel by that train without a fresh ticket, which the guard offered to procure. The pursuer, who had apparently misunderstood the reply made by the stationmaster at Aberfeldy to a question put to him when taking his ticket, declined the offer, insisting on his right to travel. He refused to leave the train, tendering his name and address, which were well known. After ten minutes delay to the train, he was forcibly removed without violence. In an action for damages and solatium [compensation] for assault and illegal removal, and for reimbursement of charges incurred for posting, it was held that the conditions under which his return ticket was issued were reasonable and duly published, that under them he was not entitled to travel on Sunday without obtaining a fresh ticket, and that on refusal to comply with the regulations, or leave the carriage, the Company were entitled to use the necessary force to remove him. Lord Ormidale, who delivered the leading judgement, observed that, "if he had no right, or, in other words, was not entitled in virtue of his ticket, to travel by train from Perth to Ballinluig, the defenders had a clear and undoubted right to insist on his leaving the carriage before the train started, and his refusal to do so occasioned such a hindrance to the company in the use of the railway as entitled them, in terms of not merely a bye-law or regulation, but of the statute itself (Sec 102 of the R. CL. Cons. Act), "summarily to interfere" to remove such hindrance.

Did the events of 1863 where Sir Robert Menzies in effect forced the construction of the branch contribute to this situation? One can only speculate. The findings of the court, do, nonetheless, put the Aberfeldy branch into the litany of classic Scottish, English and Irish court cases on the theme of fares and tickets.

Ballinluig still sold LMSR tickets in 1965, 17 years after the company disappeared. The facility for passengers to travel by goods train was available throughout the former Highland Railway territory but was rarely used. Paying first class fare to travel in a draughty brake van was not very popular! But the remaining tickets were snapped up by enthusiasts as souvenirs, such as this one issued for the final train on the branch.

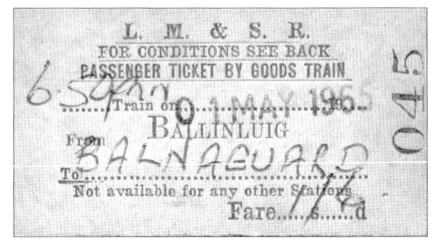

End of the Line

Various sources refer to the significant effect the branch line had on life in the area, the previously referred to *Never an Old Tin Hut* describes rapid change occurring to local society after its opening; of how several hundred locals took advantage of cheap fares to enjoy an away day on the September "Monday Holiday" and of the trainloads of day trippers in the inter-war summers being bussed to Kenmore to cruise Loch Tay to Killin thence by rail to their various industrial towns and cities. The book *Memories of an Aberfeldy Childhood* by James Fisher describes the station as being the most important point in Aberfeldy, employing in the twenties up to twenty five people, and further describing its major importance both in passenger travel and goods traffic, being the principal source of communication for these elements. Lastly *Aberfeldy Past and Present* by N.D. MacKay regarded the opening as a red letter day in the history of the village, whilst reminiscing about old carriages, he was concerned in 1952 about closure due to road competition.

Significant, important or vital could describe the branch lines' worth to the area, but like its inception in a time of great change, the 1950s and 1960s were also times of social and economic change. Post war reconstruction was still in progress and the private motor car and lorry transport was increasing. With budgets still tight and fiscal austerity demanded, Dr Beeching was brought

Even diesel locomotives needed to take on water, but only for the train heating boiler. The Highland Railway may not have provided heat in its trains on the Aberfeldy branch, but British Railways took a bit more care of its passengers, even if by January 1965 when this photograph was taken, more water was spilled on the ground than reached the locomotive. (Norris Forrest/GNSRA)

in to run the railways and reduce the losses. His report *The Re-shaping of British Railways*, better known as the Beeching Report, planned a massive reduction in route mileage and in passenger and freight services. Lines whose usage in terms of passenger numbers or freight tonnage fell below required norms were quite simply axed. Regretfully the Ballinluig to Aberfeldy branch was destined for closure under these proposals.

In the *Perthshire Advertiser* of 30th March 1963 the views of Provost James Fisher of Aberfeldy were reported as follows:-

This closure wasn't unforeseen, but it is nonetheless a serious setback for Aberfeldy. Just how serious it will be is difficult to assess and, until the alternative transport plans are known I sincerely hope that adequate provision will be made for passengers before the closure takes place.

A matter of grave concern is the future of those locally employed on the railways. Not only do the future prospects of those immediately concerned give rise to anxiety, but the loss of this source of employment is a serious one for our community.

In the same newspaper of 10th April the Church of Scotland Presbytery of Perth also expressed effects of closures on local communities, using the analogy of small country churches it was stated:-

"If you are talking profitability as the sole criterion, then we have to close down all our aid-receiving churches throughout the country".

The presbytery was of the view that they and other bodies express their grievous concern as to the implications of this.

Many local people came to see the last train arrive on Saturday 1st May 1965, due in at 7.4pm. Two coaches were provided on this train as one had come through from Perth. (Janette Adamson collection)

After the last train arrived at Aberfeldy in the evening, it would normally have remained there over the weekend ready to work the first train out at 6.35am on Monday. But on 1st May, the loco ran round the train and set off for Perth for the final time, on this occasion conveying a number of passengers who had come for a last trip on the line. Guard Willie Matheson holds up his flag, but possibly only for photographers as two doors are still open. (*Janette Adamson collection*)

A process of consultation took place, but to no avail although it was reported in the *Perthshire Advertiser* of 4th April 1964 that the map produced by British Railways showed the Aberfeldy to Crieff and Aberfeldy to Dunkeld roads along the south of the Tay as being trunk roads. The railway representative did withdraw this claim stating that they were "A" class roads; of significance nearly 50 years later is that neither of these roads have been greatly improved or modified.

The Scottish Transport Users Consultative Committee duly considered the proposed closure and heard objectors early in 1964. This body had to decide on the level of hardship which would be caused by the withdrawal of passenger services, but had no say in the future of freight facilities. The alternative bus services were explained and the bus company offered to make minor adjustments. With that the Committee concluded that no appreciable hardship would arise. An additional bus was to operate from Perth to Aberfeldy at 6.10pm and the 7.10am bus in the opposite direction was to run 5 minutes earlier to provide a better connection at Perth.

The inevitable then happened; in September 1964 the official public notice of terms of the 1962 Transport Act was published in the appropriate newspapers, etc., intimating the "WITHDRAWAL OF RAILWAY PASSENGER SERVICES BETWEEN BALLINLUIG AND ABERFELDY" at a date which will be announced by British Railways Scottish Region. There was then a delay of several months, possibly in part due to the need to get permission to run the extra bus service, before the General Manager of the Scottish Region issued on 18th March 1965 the said letter intimating that closure would take place on Monday 3rd May 1965. On that day, two months short of its centenary, the Aberfeldy branch line came to an end. At the same time Ballinluig, Dalguise and Murthly on the main line closed and the local service from Perth to Blair Atholl was withdrawn.

The goods service had already been withdrawn, on 25th January, and the impact of that was reported by the *Perthshire Advertiser*:-

Aberfeldy has already felt the effects of the local closure of railway goods traffic. Coal merchants in the town (writes the Aberfeldy correspondent) have to collect from wagons at Ballinluig junction, result – an increase in the price of coal.

Within six weeks of closure the manager, Highland Lines, Inverness, had circulated the appropriate departments in the Scottish region regarding the disposal of the "redundant assets" of the Aberfeldy branch into various categories. Months and years of design, construction, usage and maintenance were reduced to terse simple descriptions as the following examples illustrate:-

BALNAGUARD		
Shelter	Timber / corrugated iron	12' x 5' x 7'
Platform	Timber / Timber	52 yds
GRANDTULLY		
Station Building	Timber / slated	5'6" x 12'6" x 8'
Store	Asbestos / Felt	24'6" x 16' x 8'
Latrine	Timber / corrugated iron	12' x 7'6" x 8"
Coal Shed	Timber / corrugated iron	12' x 7'6" x 7'
Store	Timber / slated	19' x 15' x 7'
Crane	Timber	Capacity 3 T
Cattle pens	Timber	
Platform	Stone / stone	75 yds
Loading bank	Stone / stone	100 yds
Sidings		394 yds
ABERFELDY DISTILLERY		
Weighing machine		Capacity 32 cwt
Crane (L.M.S. 1900)	Timber	Capacity 1½ T
Sidings		566 yds
ABERFELDY		
Station building with Canopy above	Stone / slated	45' x 26' x 9'
Bookstall attached to lean-to (John Menzies & Co Ltd)	Timber / felt	13' x 8' x 3'
Latrines & stores	Stone / slated	23' x 13' 8'
Weighing machine		Capacity 30 cwt
Water tower		21' x 13' x 4'6" – 2.6 T
Base stone		20' x 12' x 14'
Signal box	Timber / slated	16'6"x 11' x 10'
Engine shed	Timber / felt	78' x 13' x 13'
Latrine	Brick / corrugated iron	6' x 4' x 7'
Weighing machine		Capacity 10 cwt
Van body		18' x 7' x 7'6"
Sawdust shed	Timber / corrugated iron	9' x 7' x 7'
Weighing cabin	Timber / corrugated iron	11' x 7' x 8'
Weighing platform		18' x 8' capacity 20T
Store	Timber / corrugated iron	12' x 10' x 8'

Crane (L.M.S. 1901)	Timber / iron	4T
Water column		12' x 1'9"
Platform	Stone / stone	123 yds
	Concrete/ Stone	16 yds
Loading bank	Stone / stone	142 yds
	Concrete / stone	50 yds
	Concrete / concrete	147 yds
	Timber / stone	95 yds
	Timber / timber	16 yds
	Cast concrete	16 yds
Sidings		2018 yds
Lengthman's Hut	Timber / corrugated iron	12' x 10'
Wagon clearance gauge		

The Tay Viaduct is similarly described:-

Viaduct	Latched steel girders	145' x 13' x 2'3" – 260T
	Steel beams 66 No	18'6" x 1'2" x 8"
	Cast iron pilasters	6 No 20" high
	Steel girders 4 No	47'6" x 3'3" x 1'4"
	Steel beams 24 No	17'2" x 1'2" x 8"
	Cast iron pilasters	2 No 12' high

The numerous masonry built bridges are described simply as stone arches.

The branch is closed, the assets removed or demolished; one can only speculate on what might have been had the closure not taken place. Of interest however was a feature contained in a national newspaper in the 1970s in which a local G.P. explained that whilst Aberfeldy and Strathtay appear to be the rural idyll, they are in fact no different from the major conurbations. Statistically he had to deal with the same percentages of illnesses, serious and otherwise, per head of population as the Scottish average. The area was in reality no different from and required the same skills and services as major cities. Consider also the thoughts of Duncan Kennedy in his book *The Birth and Death of a Highland Railway*, the story of the Ballachulish line in which he suggests that if a line is closed, in particular one

Even in the 1950s, the wooden engine shed at Aberfeldy was decrepid. Part of the roof had disappeared and the sides were shored up with timber baulks. The view from the inside on the last day of service shows how its only value by then was as firewood.
(David Stirling)

that served an outlying community, the track be maintained for a period of five years. The effect on the community and the possibility of local change or technology change should then be re-assessed, in fact he suggests that the track should not be lifted until after the succeeding general election.

Bearing these facts in mind take the subsequent discovery of Barytes (Barium Sulphate) in appreciable quantities in the hills above Aberfeldy. This substance is used extensively as a sealant in offshore oilfields. Due to transportation difficulties, neither development or mining commenced and no extraction took place; would a railhead have helped? The advent of radio controlled signalling and the development of lightweight diesel railcars would also have effected significant cost savings whilst still maintaining the vital communication link. These thoughts are, however, just that; perhaps it could have happened but it didn't. Nearly one hundred years of goods traffic, people coming and going, some never to return, are finished, and, now, nearly 50 years later are simply fond and distant memories. Appropriately, however, I shall conclude as I began. The introduction was the *Perthshire Advertiser* article on the opening of the line; it is only fitting, therefore, to end the story with the article from the same newspaper of 5th May 1965 reporting its closure:-

ABERFELDY BRANCH RAILWAY CLOSES DOWN – Nearly 100 years of railway service to Aberfeldy ended on Saturday.

In the late afternoon a crowd began to gather at the station to give the last outgoing train a send off. It was the largest gathering on the platform for many years and cameras were out in plenty, but there was no ceremony and little excitement. The train was well-filled as it left at 5.25pm to the accompaniment of a few half-hearted cheers and the explosion of detonators on the line.

At seven o'clock a slightly smaller crowd appeared on the platform to welcome the last incoming train, which had a full complement of passengers, and again cameras were much in evidence.

After the crowd dispersed the office closed down and later in the evening the engine and empty train pulled out.

Another view on the last day, showing that many locals turned out. Did they ever travel on the train?

(David Stirling)

Memories of the Final Decade

Despite what eventually ensued in 1965, the branch was still quite busy in the mid to late 1950s. Low car ownership and a poor road network meant that the principal means of transport of goods and people was still by rail. Aberfeldy Station in particular employing at any one time between 15-20 staff in a variety of positions, I am grateful, therefore to local people and those formerly resident at that time for supplying the following details. Apologies to those who have been unintentionally omitted or incorrectly described, it being nearly fifty years ago memories are somewhat faded.

The Stationmaster during that period was Mr Paterson, with the office staff of booking and goods clerks being Alfie Forbes, George Dorward and Willie Anderson. Footplate crew were drivers Dave Battison and Willie Lees along with firemen Charlie Cairney, Jock McDonald and Michael McGroarty. Guards of that era were Dave Stewart, Willie Matheson, Wattie Gordon, Ronnie Brown, with as relief Dave Cameron known affectionately as "Lochiel". Porters dealing with passengers, goods and parcels were Jock Mathieson, James Johnstone and James Mackie. Travelling daily from Dalguise by train until his marriage to a local girl was Alastair Grant, the yard driver, who delivered railway parcels firstly on an old Albion lorry and then on the classic Scammel "Scarab" three wheeler mechanical horse and trailer. Finally the permanent way crew were Andrew Morton (Ganger) and Geordie Grant, Bob McGillivary and K. Morton as platelayers/lengthmen; they had their hut next to the cattle dock and signal box where their equipment, spares and tools were stored along with the wheeled barrow used on the rails. Those staffing levels continued into the early 1960s when substantial cutbacks were introduced in the years prior to closure.

During most of this period passenger traffic was steady, rail still being a convenient and in all probability the quickest means of public transport between Aberfeldy, Pitlochry and Perth and thence to further destinations. Regular passengers also travelled from Balnaguard or Grandtully to Aberfeldy to their work in shops, hotels or Fishers laundry. Some teachers, too, travelled this way to their posts at Breadalbane Academy, the principal school of North Perthshire. Frequent use of rail was also made by Civil Defence staff making their way to Taymouth Castle in nearby Kenmore, which for many years was the Scottish H. Q. of that organisation. Holiday traffic was still around at that time, as was use of the camping coach.

One notable regular rail user of that period was the "Arbroath Fish Lady", who every Wednesday travelled from that Angus town with her creels of fresh herring, haddock and the famous "Smokie". She sold these throughout the town, pushing them around on a set of old pram wheels which were stored at the station solely for that purpose. Not surprisingly the fish were carried in the guard's van.

Probably the best known regular passenger was Chrissie McCulloch who "commuted" daily from Balnaguard accompanied by her faithful Springer spaniel "Billy". Chrissie was manager of the John Menzies bookstall at the station and whilst travelling on the first train in the morning in an empty compartment, she sorted out the various newspapers and magazines for uplift by other newsagents, onward delivery by Mailbus to Kenmore, Fortingall, Fearnan and Glenlyon or local delivery in Aberfeldy. At the station bookstall Chrissie was ably assisted by Jean Stewart, known affectionately as Jean "Benbec", a Gaelic speaking lady who hailed originally from Benbecula in the outer Hebrides. Chrissie later emigrated to California where she served as a housekeeper to an

American family; by chance some years later she met up with her former paper delivery boy Michael Dorward at San Francisco's Pier 32, where the P & O liner "Canberra" on which he served, was docked. Small world indeed!

Steady goods traffic both in and out of the area still prevailed during the mid to late 1950's, most of it regular, some occasional or seasonal. Aberfeldy Distillery would, for example, receive weekly supplies of malting barley generally from the Aberdeenshire/Morayshire areas along with routine deliveries of coal and yeast. The distillery sent out, usually on a weekly basis, wagons of spent mash, used locally for cattle feed, and would at least monthly despatch several wagonloads of barrels to the Dewar's bond in Perth. All the area's coal supplies, too, came in by rail, principally from the Fife coalfields, supplying Messrs James Lind, Crerar & McNab and A & J McDougall, the three local coal merchants. The coal was all unloaded manually from open wagons, barrowed into the various bins and then weighed and bagged into hundredweight sacks for subsequent local delivery.

Local hotels, newsagents, shops and in particular the large store of McKerchar & McNaughton obtained most of their supplies by rail, such as wines and spirits, cigarettes, drapery, household goods and supplies. Insulated containers of Walls ice cream from Edinburgh were sent in the summer months, the coolant being dry ice to preserve the contents. All mail at that time both in and out of the area was rail borne with the requirement for additional vans at the Christmas period. In those days long before the advent of satellite or electronic transmission I recall cans of film, which were no doubt heading for the Glasgow studios for processing, being put on the early evening train from a B.B.C series about the Road to the Isles fronted by that well known presenter of the period Fyfe Robertson.

The local farming community also made extensive use of the line, a significant feature being the livestock mart, the monthly sales necessitating additional wagons for onward transit of sheep or cattle. In particular the large Spring cattle sale and the late December sheep sales required special trains of up to 30-40 wagons which in turn needed heavier locomotive power, usually a Black 5. Cuil, Balhomas and Borlicks farms frequently consigned churns of milk by rail to Pitlochry for local use or to Perth to the major Perth Creamery Co. or Perth Co-operative Dairy for processing and bottling. After the introduction of its own bottling line Balhomas Farm obtained deliveries of milk bottles (in straw packed hessian sacks) along with milk bottle tops by rail. In late October and early November of each year considerable quantities of, in particular, King Edward and Majestic varieties of seed potatoes were sent out by rail generally to English markets. These potatoes would arrive at the station by lorry or tractor and trailer usually in jute sacks

A paperboy at Aberfeldy station bookstall in 1955.
(Mrs M McCulloch collection)

and then be manhandled into wagons on a bed of straw with straw also being packed around up to roof level as frost protection.

Smaller firms and individuals also benefitted from the service provided; wool was sent by local farms to grading stations in Glasgow, Bonhill, Dunfermline, Paisley and Kirkcaldy. The local firm of P & J Haggart used rail to send rolls of tweed to Border mills for dressing and then for their return along with the supply of specialist materials. The local game dealer Peter McGregor used the line to send fresh Tay salmon, grouse, venison and other game to various hotels, restaurants or shops throughout the country. Another recollection is of a local worthy and dog breeder, Miss Thompson of Tigh na Coille near Weem, who advertised pups for sale in *Exchange and Mart* and on receipt of an order would have the pups safely ensconsed in a tea chest, with straw bedding and a chicken wire cover. She placed this on a small trailer and then cycled to the station to deliver it for onward transit to its new owners.

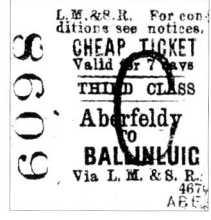

Finally in this section are personal reminiscences of people who remember the line or whose relatives worked on the railway. Mrs Liz Fischbacher, daughter of Dave Stewart a former guard, recalls her father being accompanied by hens, pigs and other young farm animals in the guard's van generally wrapped in a jute sack with merely a head sticking out. Mrs Janette Adamson, daughter of Willie Matheson (who was the guard on the last train), remembers that on occasions pheasant would be served for dinner after accidental collisions with the locomotive! Mrs Sheila Menzies, who worked in the Council Roads Office, used the station as a shortcut to her work, crossing the line after the water tank and then going up the steps to the depot, thus saving a long detour. Lastly a tale from the same lady concerning her late brother-in-law Neil, who as a student in the early 1960's cycled to the station each Monday morning to catch the first train to attend Agricultural College in Perth. Being slightly late one morning he arrived only to see the train departing; the crew looking back spotted him, promptly stopped and reversed to pick him up. Truly this was a local line serving the local community.

On the final day, 1st May 1965, the single coach train heads out of Aberfeldy in the early afternoon. This was an empty stock working. (Keith Fenwick)

Aberfeldy station from above the town on the day of closure. (David Stirling)

The sign for Balnaguard Halt survives, but even before closure it was broken in half so you have to read both sides to see the full name. The background is yellow. (C J Stewart)

The over-bridge to the west of Grandtully, which afforded a good vantage point to view the station, still stands. The trackbed towards Aberfeldy is now a footpath.
(C J Stewart)

Lasting Reminders

Nearly fifty years having elapsed since closure so it is only natural that considerable change has occurred; nonetheless evidence of the line's existence is still visible, particularly parts of the track bed.

No station sites, however, remain; Ballinluig is now covered by the upgraded flyover and junction between the re-built A9 and the A827. The adjacent Tummel viaduct was also removed during those road improvements to make way for a new road bridge on the A827. Balnaguard Halt is now used as a silage pit. The site of the station at Grandtully is now a campsite run by the Scottish Canoe Association, the rapids on the nearby River Tay having various slalom courses set out on what is regarded as one of the foremost canoeing facilities in Scotland. The support walls at the loading dock are, however, still apparent.

Aberfeldy, the largest station on the branch, has been totally removed and is now a housing estate, the only indication of previous railway activity being the bridge which led to the old County Council yard located at the eastern end of the station. The distillery, too, is similarly bereft; some evidence of the loading dock and the remains of the abutments to the bridge over the Pitilie Burn are all that remain.

Several sections of the track bed do survive. The portion commencing from the Tay viaduct at Logierait and heading westwards to Balnaguard is still basically intact and can be best viewed from the adjacent and parallel B898 road. From Balnaguard westwards no trace can be seen over the farmlands of Strathtay. It picks up again at Haugh of Grandtully and continues with several interruptions westwards to Aberfeldy. This section is however mainly through steeply sloping wooded hillsides and alongside the River Tay, illustrating clearly to any walker the considerable cuttings and embankments found on this section of the branch. This latter section is referred to in such websites as "Trail Scotland" and "Scotland's Bike Community".

Of significant interest, however, is the story of the rescue of the largest (by far) structure on the branch, the Tay Viaduct at Logierait, designed by Joseph Mitchell and built by Fairbairns of

The site of Grandtully station is now a campsite and not much remains of the railway, except for the edge of the goods platform. The track curved away to the right in the distance on its route to Ballinluig.
(C J Stewart)

Aberfeldy's Railway

Top chord of girder comprises
4 No. 4" x 4" x ¾" angles with
2 No. 12" x ¾" web plates and
2' 3" x 1¼" top flange plate.

Lattice girder comprises
4½" x 3" x ½" thick angles and
4½" x 1" thick plates on each face, braced with 4 sets of
3" x ¼" cross bracing and
8" x ¼" plates between pairs of angles

Lattice girder as other

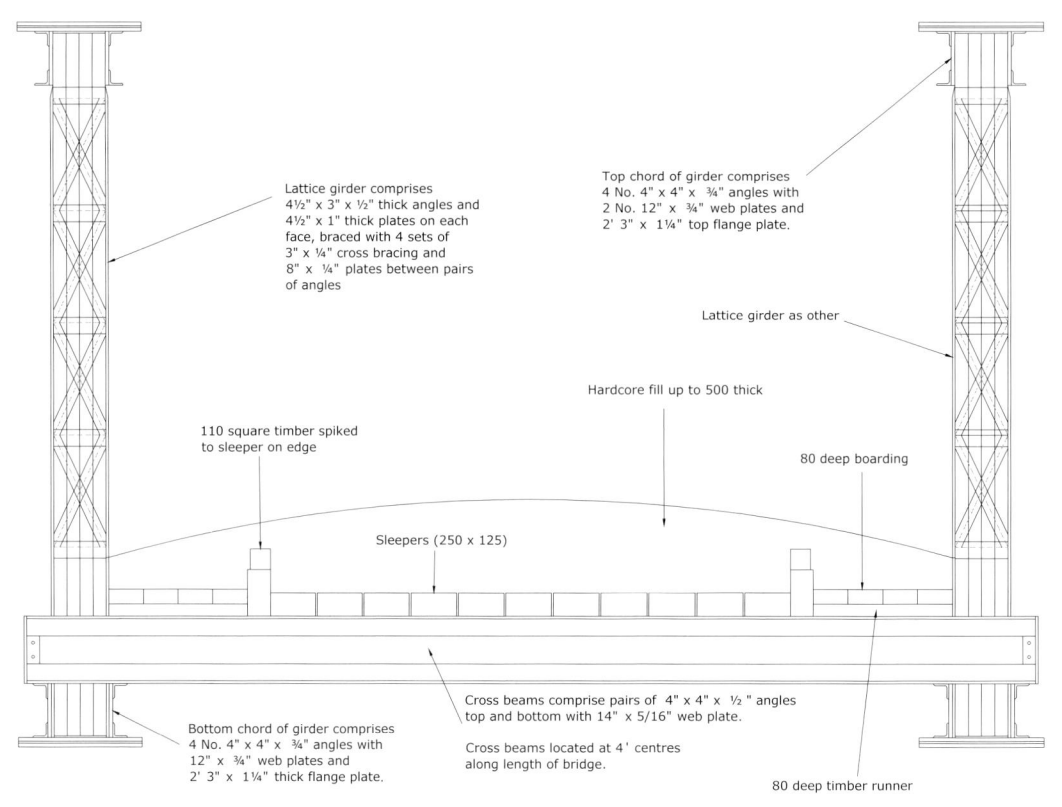

Hardcore fill up to 500 thick

110 square timber spiked to sleeper on edge

80 deep boarding

Sleepers (250 x 125)

Cross beams comprise pairs of 4" x 4" x ½" angles top and bottom with 14" x 5/16" web plate.

Cross beams located at 4' centres along length of bridge.

Bottom chord of girder comprises
4 No. 4" x 4" x ¾" angles with
12" x ¾" web plates and
2' 3" x 1¼" thick flange plate.

80 deep timber runner

These two drawings produced by Allen, Gordon & Co show cross-sections of the Tay Viaduct above as previously existing and below as proposed for the refurbishment by the Logierait Bridge Company for use as a roadway.

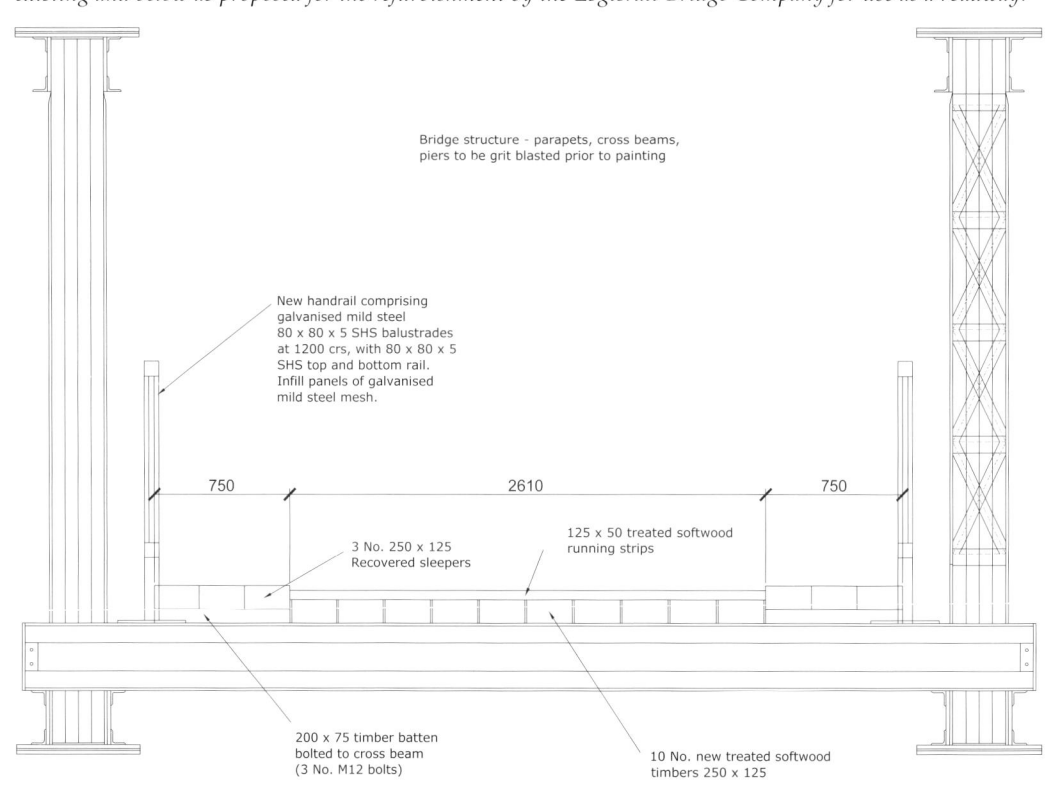

Bridge structure - parapets, cross beams, piers to be grit blasted prior to painting

New handrail comprising galvanised mild steel 80 x 80 x 5 SHS balustrades at 1200 crs, with 80 x 80 x 5 SHS top and bottom rail. Infill panels of galvanised mild steel mesh.

750   2610   750

125 x 50 treated softwood running strips

3 No. 250 x 125 Recovered sleepers

200 x 75 timber batten bolted to cross beam (3 No. M12 bolts)

10 No. new treated softwood timbers 250 x 125

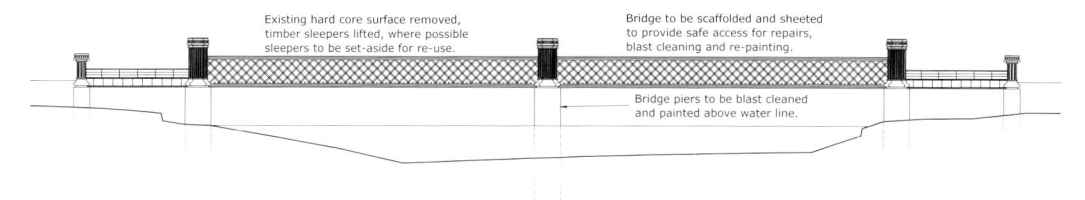

Tay Viaduct elevation, from Allen, Gordon & Co drawings.

Manchester at a cost of £13,770. The bridge is also listed by the government as being of "Historic and/or Architectural importance" in Category 1 – the highest category for preserving architecturally important structures, it being one of the few remaining lattice girder bridges in existence. It would now cost £14 million to rebuild (based on 2001 estimates). From newspaper articles and the Logierait Bridge Company it is possible to recount the events leading to its takeover and restoration.

After closure in 1965 ownership of the bridge passed to the Kinnaird estate, the bridge being used as a short cut from Dalguise, Balnaguard and neighbouring farms to access Logierait, Ballinluig and the A9, saving a detour of up to ten miles. Not surprisingly considerable maintenance was needed, in particular to the decking, and the owners attempted to get the then Tayside Regional Council to take over the bridge and the subsequent upkeep thereof. Not unsurprisingly this was refused and later in 1991 the owners attempted to shut the structure on safety grounds; this was vehemently resisted by the local community who obtained an interdict from Perth Sheriff Court that prevented it. The community then formed a charitable company entitled the Logierait Bridge Company which purchased the bridge for £1. The company raised local funding of £2,500, a sum matched by the former owners, which enabled essential repairs to be carried out. Funds were raised locally by donation with events such as ceilidhs and interestingly by the sale of water colour prints of the bridge by Sir Anthony Wheeler OBE PPRSA, illustrated on the rear cover, who gifted all rights in his painting to the bridge company.

This short term measure ensured continued use of the structure but much more was needed to satisfy long term requirements. A grant of £5,000 obtained from Perth and Kinross Heritage Trust meant that a proper and detailed survey could be undertaken and to this end Messrs Allen, Gordon and Company, a Perth based firm of Consulting Civil and Structural Engineers, were appointed. Their survey indicated that whilst the structure was essentially sound, deck replacement, painting and handrail installation were required. The all-in cost of the works including VAT and fees were approximately £400,000.

Under the inspired guidance of Robert Smith OBE of Dalguise, a former director of the Association for the Protection of Rural Scotland, funds were raised locally and considerable grants obtained from Historic Scotland, the Heritage Lottery Fund, the Scottish Parliaments Rural Challenge Fund, the Ellis Campbell Foundation and the Manifold Trust. In addition the Millennium Commission provided a grant via Sustrans, organisers of the national cycle network. This magnificent effort meant that in the autumn of 2000 work started to restore the viaduct.

Before commencement the bridge was cocooned in scaffolding and sheeting to prevent debris falling into the river. The actual works comprised deck replacement

> **THE TAY VIADUCT, LOGIERAIT**
>
> First opened in 1865 by the Inverness and Perth Junction Railway (later to become the Highland Railway), the Tay Viaduct passed into the hands of Kinnaird Estate in 1964 after the last train had crossed the bridge on 1st May of that year. In 1994 the estate gifted it to the local community which founded the Logierait Bridge Company (a company limited by guarantee with charitable status) to hold it.
>
> In 2000/01 it was comprehensively restored at a cost of around £400,000 and re-opened as a community-owned road bridge.

with 10in x 5in treated softwood sleepers each spanning over two cross beams running lengthwise over the bridge, 5in x 2in runners spaced 2in apart placed transversely on the deck, the installation of galvanised handrails to both sides (an obvious safety requirement) and repainting.

The repainting is of significance as records have indicated this had been last undertaken in 1938, a 73 year gap! In this instance all steelwork was shot blasted to bare with the piers given one coat of primer and two coats of finish, the paints being specialist epoxy coatings. All other metalwork received epoxy primer, undercoat and polyurethane finish.

Finally, on Wednesday 1st August 2001 Constance Ward of Kinnaird Estate cut the ribbon to mark the "Official Opening" of the restored structure in front of an audience of 70 – 80 people including both the MP and MSP for the area. In conclusion, it is only right and proper to reproduce the wording on the plaque on the east side of the bridge-

> The Board of the Logierait Bridge Company acknowledge the leadership and persistence of Robert L Smith OBE. His knowledge and dogged determination were instrumental in ensuring the rescue and refurbishment of the bridge in 2000/2001.

Testament indeed to a fine man, a fine structure, its original designers and builders, and a lasting reminder of what has now passed.

Two recent views of Logierait bridge. The elaborate columns are all cast iron. (C J Stewart)

BIBLIOGRAPHY

A.K. Bell Library, Perth	Various newspaper articles from the *Perthshire Advertiser*, *Perthshire Courier*.
Blair Castle Archives	Various correspondence between Railway Companies and His Grace The Duke of Athole
National Archives of Scotland, Register House	BR/IPJ/1/1-2 Inverness & Perth Junction Railway minutes
	BR/HR/1/1 et seq Highland Railway minutes
	RHP/17091/2 Plans and sections of Aberfeldy branch
	RHP/45088 Inverness & Perth Junction Railway Parliamentary Notice, Book of Reference
	BR/AP(S) – 123 Inverness & Perth Junction Railway Act
	BR-RSR-4 Closure Notices and List of Redundant assets
	GD 112 – Breadalbane Papers
H.M.S.O.	Ministry of Transport report on Balnaguard derailment
Highland Railway Society *Journal*	Various articles

Books

Aberfeldy Past and Present, N.D. McKay, Wm Culross
Highland Main Line, Neil T. Sinclair, Atlantic
Highland Railway, O.S. Nock, Ian Allan 1965
Highland Railway, H.A. Vallance, House of Lochar
Highland Railway, David Ross, Stenlake Publishiing
Highland Railway, People and Places, Neil T. Sinclair, Breedon Books
Highland Railway Locomotives, 2 vols, Cormack and Stevenson, RCTS.
Highland Railway Locomotives, Peter Tatlow, Oxford
Highland in L.M.S. Days, David Jenkinson, Pendragon
Law of Railways Applicable to Scotland, Francis Deas M.A., LLB, Advocate, William Green & Sons, Edinburgh, 1897
Never an Old Tin Hut, Jack Rees, Wm Culross
On Highland Lines, Robert Robotham, Ian Allan
Perth & Dunkeld Railway, Keith Fenwick and Neil T Sinclair, Highland Railway Society
Scottish Branch Lines, C.J. Gammel, Oxford
Tayside's Railway, Perth and Dundee, W.A.C. Smith & Paul Anderson, Irwell Press

Articles

Back Track	Jan 1996 Camping Coaches in Scottish Region, (2 articles)
	Highland Railway Tank Locomotives
Steam World	June 1991 Scottish Idyll
Steam Days	Feb 1994 Highland Railway Engine Sheds
	April 1994 The Aberfeldy Branch
	April 1996 Mid-morn Ritual at Ballinluig
	Jan 1999 Scottish region Camping Coaches
Railway Byelines	Oct 2000 Aberfeldy – ABR Miscellany
	March 2001 Aberfeldy Diesel days

Guard Willie Matheson removes the commemorative board on the rear of the last train to Aberfeldy on 1st May 1965. This was adapted from a Highland Railway 'Engine Following' board by adding 'No Train'. (Janette Adamson collection)

THE HIGHLAND RAILWAY SOCIETY

The Highland Railway Society caters for all those interested in the varied aspects of the railway, including its predecessors and its successors to the present day.

An illustrated quarterly Journal is distributed to members and contains a wide variety of articles and information. Members queries are a regular feature and details of new books, videos and models of interest are reported. The Society's publications include a series of books commemorating the 150th anniversaries of the opening of various sections of the system.

Meetings are held regularly in both Scotland and England. An annual gathering is held each September and includes a full day of talks, films, etc., as well as an opportunity to meet fellow members.

The Society has Library, Photographic and Drawing collections which are available to members. Copies of drawings are available for purchase. Modellers are well catered for. Complete kits are produced in limited runs. Specially commissioned modelling components such as axle boxes, buffers and springs are available, plus a comprehensive set of transfers to enable any Highland loco to be named.

Membership details can be found on the Society's website at www.hrsoc.org.uk.